THE RIGHT TO A
FAIR TRIAL

Other books in this series:

The Bill of Rights

THE RIGHT TO A FAIR TRIAL

Edited by Enid W. Langbert, Esq.

Bruce Glassman, *Vice President*
Bonnie Szumski, *Publisher*
Helen Cothran, *Managing Editor*
Scott Barbour, *Series Editor*

GREENHAVEN PRESS
An imprint of Thomson Gale, a part of The Thomson Corporation

THOMSON
GALE

Detroit • New York • San Francisco • San Diego • New Haven, Conn.
Waterville, Maine • London • Munich

Cover credit: © Ron Chapple/Getty Images
Peter Ehrenhaft, Collection of the Supreme Court of the United States, 52
Independence National Historical Park Collection, 30
Library of Congress, 39, 93
National Geographic, Collection of the Supreme Court of the United States, 77
North Wind Picture Archives, 35
Photograph by Joseph D. Lavenburg, National Geographic Society, Collection of the Supreme Court of the United States, 60

LIBRARY OF CONGRESS CATALOGING-IN-PUBLICATION DATA

The right to a fair trial / Enid W. Langbert, book editor.
    p. cm. — (Bill of Rights)
Includes bibliographical references and index.
ISBN 0-7377-1939-7 (lib. : alk. paper)
    1. Fair trial—United States—History. I. Langbert, Enid W. II. Bill of Rights (San Diego, Calif.)

KF4765.R54 2005
347.73'53—dc22   2004054144

Chapter 2: Balancing the Right to a Fair Trial Against the Interests of Society

Chapter 3: Recent Controversies Regarding the Right to a Fair Trial

"I cannot agree with those who think of the Bill of Rights as an 18th century straightjacket, unsuited for this age. . . . The evils it guards against are not only old, they are with us now, they exist today."

—Hugo Black, associate justice of the
U.S. Supreme Court, 1937–1971

The Bill of Rights codifies the freedoms most essential to American democracy. Freedom of speech, freedom of religion, the right to bear arms, the right to a trial by a jury of one's peers, the right to be free from cruel and unusual punishment—these are just a few of the liberties that the Founding Fathers thought it necessary to spell out in the first ten amendments to the U.S. Constitution.

While the document itself is quite short (consisting of fewer than five hundred words), and while the liberties it protects often seem straightforward, the Bill of Rights has been a source of debate ever since its creation. Throughout American history, the rights the document protects have been tested and reinterpreted. Again and again, individuals perceiving violations of their rights have sought redress in the courts. The courts in turn have struggled to decipher the original intent of the founders as well as the need to accommodate changing societal norms and values.

The ultimate responsibility for addressing these claims has fallen to the U.S. Supreme Court. As the highest court in the nation, it is the Supreme Court's role to interpret the Constitution. The Court has considered numerous cases in which people have accused government of impinging on their rights. In the process, the Court has established a body of case law and precedents that have, in a sense, defined the Bill of Rights. In doing so, the Court has often reversed itself and introduced new ideas and approaches that have altered the legal meaning of the rights contained in the Bill of Rights. As a general rule, the Court has erred on the side of caution, upholding and expanding the rights of individuals rather than restricting them.

An example of this trend is the definition of cruel and unusual punishment. The Eighth Amendment specifically states, "Excessive bail shall not be required, nor excessive fines imposed, nor cruel and unusual punishments inflicted." However, over the years the Court has had to grapple with defining what constitutes "cruel and unusual punishment." In colonial America, punishments for crimes included branding, the lopping off of ears, and whipping. Indeed, these punishments were considered lawful at the time the Bill of Rights was written. Obviously, none of these punishments are legal today. In order to justify outlawing certain types of punishment that are deemed repugnant by the majority of citizens, the Court has ruled that it must consider the prevailing opinion of the masses when making such decisions. In overturning the punishment of a man stripped of his citizenship, the Court stated in 1958 that it must rely on society's "evolving standards of decency" when determining what constitutes cruel and unusual punishment. Thus the definition of cruel and unusual is not frozen to include only the types of punishment that were illegal at the time of the framing of the Bill of Rights; specific modes of punishment can be rejected as society deems them unjust.

Another way that the Courts have interpreted the Bill of Rights to expand individual liberties is through the process of "incorporation." Prior to the passage of the Fourteenth Amendment, the Bill of Rights was thought to prevent only the federal government from infringing on the rights listed in the document. However, the Fourteenth Amendment, which was passed in the wake of the Civil War, includes the words, ". . . nor shall any state deprive any person of life, liberty, or property, without due process of law; nor deny to any person within its jurisdiction the equal protection of the laws." Citing this passage, the Court has ruled that many of the liberties contained in the Bill of Rights apply to state and local governments as well as the federal government. This process of incorporation laid the legal foundation for the civil rights movement—most specifically the 1954 *Brown v. Board of Education* ruling that put an end to legalized segregation.

As these examples reveal, the Bill of Rights is not static. It truly is a living document that is constantly being reinterpreted and redefined. The Bill of Rights series captures this vital aspect of one of America's most cherished founding texts. Each volume in the series focuses on one particular right protected in the Bill of Rights. Through the use of primary and secondary sources, the right's evolution is traced from colonial times to the present. Primary sources include landmark Supreme Court rulings, speeches by prominent experts, and editorials. Secondary sources include historical analyses, law journal articles, book excerpts, and magazine articles. Each book also includes several features to facilitate research, including a bibliography, an annotated table of contents, an annotated list of relevant Supreme Court cases, an introduction, and an index. These elements help to make the Bill of Rights series a fascinating and useful tool for examining the fundamental liberties of American democracy.

The criminal justice system must strike a balance between two equally important but often competing values: the safety of the community and the rights of the accused. In order to ensure public safety, society must contend with individuals who break the rules and disregard the rights of others. At the same time, in a just society, those accused and convicted of crimes must be dealt with fairly and humanely. The framers of the Constitution, leery of the history of citizens' mistreatment under monarchal governments, were primarily concerned with the rights of the accused. In the Bill of Rights the framers sought to protect the individual facing criminal sanction by creating the most comprehensive limitations on governmental powers ever drafted.

Four of the ten amendments contained in the Bill of Rights deal with criminal procedure: the Fourth, Fifth, Sixth, and Eighth amendments. They impose limits on the police and the prosecutor at every stage of criminal procedure, including suspicion, arrest, trial, and sentencing. The Sixth Amendment, which sets forth the requirements for a fair criminal trial, is the pivotal criminal procedure amendment, since it is at trial that overly zealous police practices can be corrected and unfair penalties can be prevented. The Sixth Amendment enumerates eight distinct and separate rights. Four of the rights pertain to the conduct of a trial: A trial must be speedy, be public, be argued before an impartial jury, and take place in the district in which the crime occurred. The other four rights are prerogatives of the accused: The accused must be informed of the charges against them, be confronted by their accusers, be given the opportunity to call witnesses in their favor, and be assisted by counsel.

Incorporation of the Sixth Amendment

The Sixth Amendment, like all the other amendments contained in the Bill of Rights, originally applied only to the federal government. While the federal government was forbidden to impinge on the rights outlined in the Bill of Rights, each state was free to determine the scope of rights it would provide to its citizens. Following the passage of the Fourteenth Amendment, in the wake of the Civil War, the Supreme Court gradually began to apply the Bill of Rights to the states. The Fourteenth Amendment states in part:

> No State shall make or enforce any law which shall abridge the privileges or immunities of citizens of the United States; nor shall any State deprive any person of life, liberty, or property, without due process of law; nor deny to any person within its jurisdiction the equal protection of the laws.

The due process clause of the Fourteenth Amendment was interpreted by later Supreme Court justices to mean that state governments, as well as the federal government, were obligated to ensure the rights outlined in the Bill of Rights. This process of applying the Bill of Rights to the states is referred to as "incorporation." Rather than incorporating all of the rights protected by the Bill of Rights, the Court has gradually incorporated many of them in a process known as "selective incorporation." It has conducted a case-by-case examination to determine which rights are "fundamental" rights to be protected against state as well as federal action.

For almost a century after passage of the Fourteenth Amendment, the Supreme Court ignored the rights of criminal defendants—until the appointment of Justice Earl Warren, who served as chief justice of the Court from 1953 to 1969. Since then all the Sixth Amendment rights have been incorporated. One of the most significant of the Warren Court decisions was the 1963 case *Gideon v. Wainwright*, in which the Court held that the right to counsel was a fundamental right and that counsel must be appointed for any indigent defendant charged with a felony in a state proceeding.

The Right to Counsel

Despite the importance that is now placed on it, the right to counsel does not have as long a history as other Sixth

Amendment rights, such as the right to a jury trial or to a public trial. In Great Britain, defendants accused of felonies other than treason were not entitled to lawyers until 1836, and that tradition carried over to the colonies. However, by the time of independence, most state constitutions provided for a right to counsel in order to correct the imbalance of power between the accused and the public prosecutor. Defendants were entitled to retain counsel of their choice at their own expense. There was no concept of assigned counsel for those unable to afford a lawyer.

The law remained unchanged until the 1932 case *Powell v. Alabama*, popularly called the case of the "Scottsboro Boys." The Supreme Court reviewed the conviction, in an Alabama court, of nine black youths who had been charged with raping two white women. The flagrant unfairness of the Alabama court proceedings had attracted national attention. Nine separate trials had been held in one day, with counsel appointed for each defendant on the morning of trial. In overturning the youths' convictions, the Supreme Court found that their representation by assigned counsel, given no opportunity to prepare, had been a sham. The Court held that the right to counsel implied both the right to have counsel appointed and the right to have effective assistance of counsel.

The Scottsboro defendants had been sentenced to death. Following the *Powell* decision, a question remained as to whether the right to have counsel assigned in state proceedings applied to less serious crimes. Thirty years later, Clarence Gideon was charged with breaking into a poolroom. He claimed that he was entitled to counsel under the Sixth Amendment. The trial court rejected his claim, asserting that the Sixth Amendment did not apply to the states. Gideon tried the case himself, even conducting an examination of himself on the witness stand. He was convicted.

From prison, Gideon sent a handwritten petition to the Supreme Court, stating that he had wrongly been denied his right to counsel under the Sixth Amendment. The Court receives many prison petitions every year and accepts less than 1 percent of them for review. It accepted Gideon's petition and appointed a famous attorney, Abe Fortas, to argue for Gideon.

The Court unanimously overturned Gideon's conviction, saying, "In our adversary system of criminal justice, any person haled into court who is too poor to hire a lawyer, cannot be assured of a fair trial unless counsel is provided for him. That seems to us to be an obvious truth." Granted a new trial, in which he was represented by counsel, Gideon was acquitted.

The way in which a society treats those accused of violating the rules is one measure of its morality The *Gideon* decision, one of the most popular ever rendered by the Supreme Court, affirmed America's commitment to the fair treatment of criminal suspects. By ensuring, to the best of its ability, that a defendant receives a fair trial, society upholds the ideals espoused by the authors of the Bill of Rights.

CHAPTER ONE

The Historic Development of the Right to a Fair Trial

The Bill of Rights

The Origins of Trial by Jury

William Forsyth

William Forsyth was a nineteenth-century British lawyer
and law professor. In the following excerpt from his comprehensive history of the origins of trial by jury in England, he
describes the evolution of the use of juries in England during the Middle Ages. Prior to the twelfth century, accused
persons were subject to trial by oath, ordeal, or battle. In the
1100s and 1200s, these practices began to fall away. In their
place the precursors of today's grand jury and petit jury systems arose in which groups of citizens were impaneled to
bring charges and assess guilt.

The rise and growth of the Jury system is a subject which
ought to interest not only the lawyer but all who value
the institutions of England, of which this is one of the most
remarkable, being until recently a distinctive feature of our
jurisprudence.

In the following pages an attempt is made to investigate
its origin and trace its history, until it assumed the well-
defined form and office with which we are so familiar, but
which long excited the admiration and envy of the nations of
Europe, until at last, by slow degrees and to a partial extent,
many of them have succeeded in adopting it themselves. The
inquiry is more difficult than may at first sight appear. Trial
by Jury does not owe its existence to any positive law:—it is
not the creature of an Act of Parliament establishing the
form and defining the functions of the new tribunal. It arose,
as I hope to show, silently and gradually, out of the usages of
a state of society which has forever passed away, but of which

William Forsyth, *The History of Trial by Jury, Second Edition.* Jersey City, NJ: Frederick D. Linn & Company, 1875.

it is necessary to have a clear idea, in order to understand how this mode of trial first came into existence. . . .

European vs. English Juries

Sufficient attention has not been paid to what is the distinctive characteristic of the system; namely, that the Jury consists of a body of men taken from the community at large, summoned to find the truth of disputed facts, who are quite distinct from the judges or court. Their office is to decide upon the effect of evidence, and thus inform the court truly upon the question at issue, in order that the latter may be enabled to pronounce a right judgment. But they are not the court itself, nor do they form part of it; and they have nothing to do with the sentence which follows the delivery of their verdict. Moreover, they are not members of any class or corporation, on whom, as distinct from the rest of their fellow-citizens, is imposed the task of taking part in judicial inquiries. They are called upon to serve as the particular occasion arises, and then return to their usual avocations and pursuits, so as to be absolutely free from any professional bias or prejudice.

Few writers, when speculating on the rise of the jury, have kept this principle of its being separate from the court and employed solely to determine questions of fact, steadily in view. They have generally confounded the jurors with the court, and have thus imagined an identity between the former and those ancient tribunals of Europe where a select number of persons—often twelve—were taken from the community and appointed to try causes, but who did so in the capacity of Judges, and when satisfied of the evidence awarded and pronounced the doom. . . .

Far otherwise has been the case in England. Here the jury never usurped the functions of the judge. They were originally called in to aid the court with information upon questions of fact, in order that the law might be properly applied; and this has continued to be their province to the present day. The utility of such an office is felt in the most refined as well as in the simplest state of jurisprudence. Twelve men of average understanding are at least as competent now as they were in the days of Henry II. to determine whether there is sufficient evidence to satisfy them that a murder has been committed, and that the party charged with the crime is guilty. The increased technicality of the law does not affect their fitness to decide on the effect of proofs.

Hence it is that the English jury flourishes still in all its pristine vigor, while what are improperly called the old juries of the continent have either sunk into decay or been totally abolished. . . .

Ancient Forms of Justice

In considering the judicial system of the Anglo-Saxons incidental mention was made of their manner of trial in criminal cases. The accused had to clear himself by compurgation [the oaths of other people who declare him innocent] and if this failed, owing to his being unable to obtain the requisite number of persons prepared to swear to their belief in his oath of innocence, he was obliged to undergo the ordeal, which consisted of hot iron, boiling water, or the corsnaed ["the ordeal of the accused morsel," in which the accused was forced to swallow a pice of bread while his accusers prayed that it choke him if he was guilty]. We find no trace of anything like a jury empaneled to try offenders before the time of the Normans.[1] Nor for many years after the Conquest do the scanty notices which occur in the old chronicles of persons convicted and punished for crime, furnish a hint of the existence of such a tribunal. The only modes of trial in such cases of which Glanvill [a legal treatise dated 1188] speaks, are the judicial combat, compurgation, and the ordeal of hot iron where the suspected person was a freeman, and of water where he was a "villian." The judicial combat took place where an accuser came forward to make the charge; and compurgation, or the ordeal, where the accusation rested, not on the assertion of a single prosecutor, but on the *fama publica* [reputation] of the neighborhood. . . .

With respect to the accusation of criminals amongst the Anglo-Saxons, the law of Ethelred [king of England, 978–1016]

---

1. the Norman Conquest of England in 1066

has been previously noticed, which imposed upon the twelve senior thanes of each hundred the duty of discovering and presenting the perpetrators of all crimes within their district. They were to act the part of public prosecutors, and the accused had to clear himself by the usual method of compurgation, failing which, he must submit to the ordeal. This office, however, seems to have fallen into abeyance, at all events after the invasion of the Normans; and accusations of crime were left to the general voice of the neighborhood denouncing the guilt of the suspected person.

The Role of the Community

It was a consequence of the peculiar system of society in England in early times, that system which by the institution of the frithborh[2] rendered every man a surety for the conduct of his neighbor, and, therefore, responsible to a certain extent for offenses committed by him, that each community had a direct interest in discovering and bringing to justice malefactors. Besides, who were so likely to know the character of a man as his neighbors? who was so likely to be guided aright in their suspicions as to the author of a crime committed amongst themselves? Still, however, the inconvenience must have been felt of trusting to public rumors to indicate the criminal. It might be too vague and indefinite to warrant the apprehension of anyone—and different persons might entertain and express different suspicions. Or again, parties might be fearful or unwilling to make themselves conspicuous as accusers, especially after the introduction of trial by battle, which compelled them to support their charge by single combat. Accordingly we find that this led to legislative interference. The constitutions of Clarendon (A.D. 1164) provided that where a party was suspected whom no one dared openly to accuse, the sheriff, on the requisition of the bishop, should swear twelve lawful men of the neighborhood or vill [village], in the presence of the bishop, and these were "to declare the truth thereof according to their conscience." This seems evidently to mean, not only that the twelve jurors were to dis-

2. "peace-pledge," the mutual guarantee by each family to maintain the public peace

charge the office of accusers, from which private individuals had shrunk, but also to try the truth of the accusation, and pronounce upon the guilt or innocence of the accused. The *two* functions, however, in early times were almost if not altogether identical. . . . The office of accusers and triers originally led to the same result, namely, the judgment of God by the ordeal, to which the accused was remitted as the decisive test of his innocence or guilt. . . .

The Decline of the Ordeal

But the ordeal was now falling into disuse. The clergy had declared against it; and in the third year of the reign of Henry III. [1216–1272] the justices in eyre [justices who traveled through different districts] for the northern counties were ordered not to try persons charged with crime by the judgment of fire or water. Soon afterwards it so wholly disappeared, that [English legal expert Henry de] Bracton, who wrote his treatise [*On the Laws and Customs of England*] in that reign, makes no allusion to the subject.

At a parliament held at Clarendon in the reign of Henry II. [1154–1189] it was enacted that if any one were accused of murder, robbery, arson, coining, or harboring of felons, by the oaths of twelve knights of the hundred, or in default of knights, by the oaths of twelve free and lawful men, and of four men of each vill of the hundred, he was to undergo the water-ordeal, and if the result of that was unfavorable, he was to lose a foot. But even though successful at the ordeal, if he had been accused of murder or any grievous felony "by the community of the county, and the lawful knights of the county" [the commune comitatus], . . . he was obliged nevertheless to leave the kingdom within forty days, and abjure the realm. Here we see what a weighty effect was given to an accusation by the country, which to a certain extent countervailed even the proof of innocence afforded by the ordeal. It proves also how much the confidence of the leading men of the nation in the efficacy of that mode of trial was shaken, since they felt that it was safer to remove from the kingdom those who were pointed out by common fame as guilty of atrocious crimes, even although the ordeal declared them innocent.

The accusation by the commune comitatus was nothing more than the knowledge of the neighborhood, which was constantly invoked to decide questions of disputed right, applied to criminal cases, and the Statutes of Clarendon merely threw the responsibility upon a smaller number. The form of proceeding was soon afterwards modified by an ordinance of Richard I. (A.D. 1194), which provided that four knights should be chosen for each county, who when duly sworn were to choose two for each hundred or wapentake.[3] These took a similar oath, and each pair chose ten knights, or in default of knights, ten "lawful and free men," out of each hundred or wapentake so that the twelve might present the crimes and arrest the criminals within their district.

In the reign of Edward I. [1272–1307] the bailiffs of each bailiwick [jurisdiction], in order to be ready for the periodical circuits of the justices in eyre, were required to choose four knights, who again were to choose twelve of the better men of the bailiwick, and it was the duty of the latter to present all those who were suspected of having committed crimes. Each of them took the following oath: "Hear this, ye Justices! that I will speak the truth of that which ye shall ask of me on the part of the king, and I will do faithfully to the best of my endeavor. So help me God, and these holy Apostles."

A list was then put into their hands, or they were informed by the justices of the crimes and offenses of which they were to take cognizance, and they were charged to answer truly and faithfully and openly on all the matters respecting them.

In consequence of the oath which they took they were called the *jurata patriæ*, or often simply *juratores*, and for a long time seem to have united the two functions of a grand jury to accuse, and a petit jury to try the accused. It was also their duty to present any cases of suspicious death which occurred within their jurisdiction, especially where no one came forward to "appeal," *i.e.,* accuse another as the perpetrator, or if the person suspected had fled from justice, and was not forthcoming to meet the charge. . . .

3. A wapentake was a subdivision of a shire consisting of one hundred persons.

The Rise of the Trial Jury

I do not think it is possible to determine the exact period when the change took place, whereby a person accused of a crime by the inquest of the hundred was entitled to have the fact tried by another and different [jury]. Most probably there was no sudden alteration in the system, but in proportion as compurgation and the ordeal fell into disrepute, the necessity would be felt of substituting some other mode of determining whether the accusation of the jurors representing the patria was well founded or not. No tribunal would seem so proper for this purpose as one similar to that which made the charge, for the advantage would thus be secured of having the fact tried by neighbors who were most likely to know all the circumstances of the case. And even in Glanvill's time we find that a "jury of the country" was employed to determine by their testimony or verdict, whether a suspected person had fled, and been arrested after hue and cry raised. If so, he was compelled to clear himself by the *legitima purgatio*, or compurgation by witnesses. In some such way as this I conceive that trial by jury in criminal cases may have originated, and it certainly was in operation at the time when Bracton wrote, in the reign of Henry III. But even then the same jury sometimes discharged both functions of accusers and triers. . . .

At first, even after the principle was admitted that the trial of offenses fell within the cognizance of a jury, the accused was not entitled to it as a matter of right, but rather by the king's grace and favor, to be purchased by the payment of a certain sum of money or a gift of chattels, the value of which varied according to the circumstances of the case. . . .

In the time of Bracton, that is, about the middle of the thirteenth century, the usual mode of determining innocence or guilt was by combat on appeal. But in most cases the appellee had the option of either fighting with his adversary or putting himself upon his country for trial. Where, however, murder was committed by secret poisoning, the party accused of the crime was in general not allowed to choose the latter alternative, but was compelled, if he denied the charge, to defend himself by combat; "because," says Bracton, "the country can know nothing of the fact." But in some cases of this kind the appellee was allowed to make his election, and the reason assigned by Bracton is, that this was of necessity, on account of the inconvenience which would ensue if a man were always obliged to defend himself against the charge by mortal combat; for in a case of secret poisoning the accuser might have to employ a hired champion to fight for him (there being no witness of the deed whom he could put forward), which could not be allowed.

Presumed Guilty

And there were some presumptions of guilt which the law regarded as conclusive, and would not allow to be rebutted. For instance, if a man were found standing over a dead body with a bloody knife in his hand he was estopped from denying that he had murdered him; and could neither clear himself by combat nor put himself upon the country. So also in the case of a man found murdered in a house where he had slept, whose inmates made no hue and cry, and could show no wounds or other marks of violence sustained by them in defending him from the assassin.

It is obvious that this rule of regarding certain appearances against the accused not merely as presumptions, but as conclusive evidences of guilt, indicates a very defective system of jurisprudence, and must have often led to acts of gross injustice. Of all kinds of evidence that which is called circumstantial requires to be examined with the most searching care, and ought to be acted upon with the most hesitating caution. It has been often said, that circumstances can not lie; but the application of this maxim frequently involves a practical fallacy. The circumstances themselves, if proved, must, of course, be taken to be true, but their real bearing upon the question of innocence or guilt depends wholly upon the aspect in which they are viewed in relation to the accused. The appearance of a picture varies to the eye according to the light in which it is placed and the point of view from which the spectator beholds it, and yet the painting remains all the while the same. So the inference to be drawn from admitted facts, with reference to the guilt or innocence of a party, varies according to the explanation which can be given of the relation in which he actually stands towards them; but the rule of law in Bracton's time prevented the accused from giving this explanation, and the consequence must have been in many cases judicial murder. The annals of the criminal jurisprudence of all countries abound in examples of mistaken inferences of guilt.

It seems, however, there in some cases where the circumstances raised a violent presumption of guilt, the justices might direct an inquiry by a jury, although Bracton says it would be scarcely possible for the accused to escape conviction, on account of the strong presumption against him. And in answer to the objection, that he can not be pronounced not guilty of a deed done so secretly that the country can know nothing of the matter, he says that the country (*i.e.*, the jury) sufficiently acquits when it does not expressly convict.

Trial Juries Separate from Accusers

If the accused person put himself upon a jury for trial he was not allowed to choose the patria of any hundred he preferred, but the justices assigned for the purpose any set of twelve they pleased from amongst those who represented each hundred. [English jurist John] Reeves assumes that these were identical with the juries who presented the crimes and offenses of their respective districts. He says [in *History of the English Law*], "Here, then, do we see the office of the twelve jurors chosen out of each hundred at the eyre: they were to digest and mature the accusations of crimes founded upon report and the notorious evidence of the fact; and then again, under the direction of the justices, they were to reconsider their verdict, and upon such review of the matter they were to give their verdict finally."

But I incline to think that this view is incorrect, and that in the account which Bracton gives of the mode of proceeding we recognize the existence of a second and different jury, as the triers of the truth of the charge brought by the presentment of the country (fama patriæ) against the accused.

But whether this was so or not in Bracton's time, it is quite clear that the separation of the accusing from the trying jury existed in the reign of Edward III., for a statute of that monarch provides that "no indictor shall be put in inquests upon deliverance of the indictees of felonies or trespass, if he be challenged for such cause by him who is indicted.". . .

In the reign of Edward III. trials by jury in criminal cases were nearly if not quite the same as at the present day. . . .

Although the qualifications of previous knowledge on the part of jurors empaneled to try a prisoner had long fallen into desuetude, the fiction was still kept up by requiring them to be summoned from the hundred where the crime was alleged to have been committed, until the passing of Stat. 6, Geo. IV. c. 50, by which the sheriff is now obliged only to return for the trial of any issue, whether civil or criminal, twelve good and lawful men of the body of his county qualified according to law.

The Creation of the Sixth Amendment Right to a Fair Trial

R. Carter Pittman

R. Carter Pittman, an authority on the Bill of Rights and constitutional law, was a member of the Georgia Board of Bar Examiners and the author of many articles in the field of constitutional law and history. In the following selection he describes the process by which the right to a fair trial was included in the Sixth Amendment of the U.S. Bill of Rights. He concludes that the rights protected by the Sixth Amendment are fundamental to democracy. Liberty is at risk under any government that has the power to take unfair advantage of the accused by denying them a fair trial.

Liberty can not long exist under any government that is not effectively forbidden to take unfair advantages of an accused. The controls of government are always more difficult than government controls. Government powers must be divided and subdivided and limited in order that citizens may have safety and happiness, which is the primary end of all governments. The Fifth, Sixth and Eighth Amendments of the federal Bill of Rights were designed to seize the heavy hands of federal power, to catalogue and to put beyond the reach of government the most essential rights of those accused by the federal government. . . .

The Bill of Rights does not purport to create or establish rights. It shields pre-existing rights. These rights are the gift of God not governments. Each separate provision is a little foxhole of liberty ground into the hard cold face of history by

R. Carter Pittman, "The Safeguards of the Sixth Amendment," www.jtl.org.

helpless men in an effort to shield their naked bodies from the lash of tyrants.

The Rights Protected

In order to preserve liberty, we must know its history, analyze it, find its roots and sacrifice to retain it. The arithmetician proves his multiplication by division, and his subtraction by addition. Those who love liberty and wish to preserve it should carefully observe the methods used by those who wish to suppress it. Every liberty catalogued in the federal Bill of Rights could be the subject of a long historical commentary showing that each in its turn has been attacked and suppressed by those who have wanted to exercise unrestrained power.

The Sixth Amendment preserves the rights of an accused: (1) to a speedy and public trial; (2) by an impartial jury of the area wherein the crime shall have been committed; (3) to be informed of the nature and cause of the accusation; (4) to be confronted with the witnesses against him; (5) to have compulsory process for bringing his witnesses to court, and (6) to have the assistance of counsel for his defense.

The history of each of these safeguards is an appendix to the history of despotism. Each is the unwanted child of tyranny. As one reviews them history seems to pass in review. We are reminded of years spent in dungeons by martyrs to our liberty; of secret trials by servile judges, or partial juries sometimes called from afar and often called from the very household of the tyrant who headed the state; of those accused being put on trial without being informed as to the nature and cause of the accusation against them; of whispered and groundless gossip that was often the cause of the accusation; of witnesses for the accused frightened away or intimidated, leaving the accused helpless and devoid of means to compel their attendance; of a friendless accused trying to defend himself against a trained tool of arbitrary power before a judge whose daily bread depended upon the smiles of his sovereign without the assistance of counsel for his defense.

For brief illustrative treatment, let us consider the command of the Sixth Amendment that all trials of an accused be by an impartial jury: That right is often sneered at now. Yet every great constitutional document from Magna Charta to the federal Bill of Rights reaffirmed the right of the people to be tried by impartial juries of their peers. A principal cause of the Puritan Revolution and the Glorious Revolution in England, and of the American Revolution, was that those in power had poisoned the streams of justice. The Declaration of Independence indicted George III "for depriving us in many cases of the benefit of trial by jury." . . .

Impartial Juries Are Essential to Freedom

The very first step toward despotism is to establish courts that can be rigged and juries that can be stacked by those in power to effectuate their will and policies, which they always affirm to be "best for the country."

We still hear an accused put himself "on the country." That means that he puts his case and fate in the hands of a jury. Jurors were justly known to the common law as "the country." A jury represents country not government. A jury judges facts with the feelings of men who must live under government not with the impatience and passion of those who seek to administer government as if they own it. Impartial juries are essential to freedom, just as partial judges or juries are essentials to despotism.

The other safeguards of the Sixth Amendment attained constitutional status in America long before the federal Bill of Rights. The Sixth Amendment, like practically all of the other provisions of the federal Bill of Rights was written by George Mason, neighbor and mentor of George Washington in the last days of May 1776, more than a month before the Declaration of Independence. It was embodied, with few changes, in the official Virginia Declaration of Rights adopted on June 12, 1776, three weeks before the Declaration of Independence. As originally written it embodied in its paragraph 10 every provision of the Sixth Amendment except that relating to assistance by counsel.

Mason proposed a Bill of Rights in the Federal Constitutional Convention of 1787. The rejection of his proposal by the unanimous votes of the states represented embittered him and his bitterness embittered others against him and thus the one who preserved for us the fruits of martyrdoms became a martyr himself in the same cause.

A few untold details as to the genesis of the Sixth Amendment, not heretofore revealed, may interest someone. The original of George Washington's famous letter to James Madison, dated October 10, 1787, recently uncovered in New England and not yet published, differs materially from the Letter Book copy which is the only one ever published. When it is published and when the Jasper Yeates *Notes of Debates in the Pennsylvania Ratifying Convention*, recently uncovered, are published it will appear, in those new lights that Mason prepared essential parts of the draft of a Bill of Rights proposed by a minority in the Pennsylvania Ratifying Convention a few weeks after the Federal Convention adjourned: Those provisions shielding an accused from the crushing power of the new and untried government were written in the same words used by Mason in Williamsburg in May, 1776.

George Mason

An Iron Curtain Protecting Liberty

After Mason returned to Virginia he was chosen a delegate to the Virginia Ratifying Convention. Early in that Convention he was circulating a proposed federal Bill of Rights which was subsequently adopted with slight changes for proposal to the First Congress by the Virginia Ratifying Convention in late June 1788. Copies of Mason's proposals were sent to New York on June 9, 1788, and to North Carolina and to Rhode Island also. The conventions of all four states adopted Mason's draft with only slight changes. . . .

The Sixth Amendment was No. 8 in Mason's draft as follows:

That in all capital or criminal Prosecutions, a man hath a right to demand the cause and nature of his accusation, to be confronted with the accusers and witnesses, to call for Evidence and be admitted counsel in his Favor, and to a fair and speedy Trial by an impartial Jury of his vicinage, without whose unanimous consent he cannot be found guilty, (except in the Government of the land and naval Forces in Time of actual war, Invasion or Rebellion) nor can he be compelled to give Evidence against himself.

Mason's draft of proposals with which the First Congress was bombarded by Virginia, New York, North Carolina and Rhode Island in 1789 became the matrix of the federal Bill of Rights adopted on December 15, 1791. Every element of the Sixth Amendment was copied almost verbatim from Mason's 8th proposal. They constitute an iron curtain between the liberty of the individual and the arbitrary power of rulers acting in the name of the state.

The Right to a Speedy Trial Is a Fundamental Right

Earl Warren

The Sixth Amendment limits the power of the federal government by enumerating the rights of people accused of a crime. The Fourteenth Amendment, passed after the Civil War, extends these limitations to state governments to prevent them from violating the rights of people accused of a crime. However, the Fourteenth Amendment does not enumerate the rights protected, as the Sixth Amendment does, but instead describes the prohibitions. Under the Fourteenth Amendment, the states are prohibited from "abridging the privileges and immunities of citizens" and from denying them "due process of the law" and "equal protection of the laws." This language has required interpretation by the courts to determine whether particular state laws violate the Fourteenth Amendment.

The following selection is excerpted from the Supreme Court decision in *Klopfer v. North Carolina*. Klopfer's trial for criminal trespass in North Carolina had ended in a mistrial. The prosecutor sought a "nolle prosequi with leave," a procedural device that, under North Carolina law, allowed the accused to go free but to remain subject to prosecution at any time in the future at the discretion of the prosecutor. The Supreme Court, in a decision written by Chief Justice Earl Warren, held that the North Carolina statute was unconstitutional because it violated Klopfer's right to a speedy trial, an ancient and fundamental right.

Warren was chief justice of the Supreme Court from 1953 to 1969. He is best remembered for authoring the landmark *Brown v. Board of Education* (1954) decision outlawing school segregation.

Earl Warren, majority opinion, *Klopfer v. North Carolina,* 1967.

Petitioner's trial on a North Carolina criminal trespass indictment ended with a declaration of a mistrial when the jury failed to reach a verdict. After the case had been postponed for two terms, petitioner filed a motion with the trial court in which he petitioned the court to ascertain when the State intended to bring him to trial. While this motion was being considered, the State's prosecutor moved for permission to take a "nolle prosequi with leave," a procedural device whereby the accused is discharged from custody but remains subject to prosecution at any time in the future at the discretion of the prosecutor. . . .

On appeal to the Supreme Court of North Carolina, petitioner contended that the entry of the nolle prosequi with leave order deprived him of his right to a speedy trial as required by the Fourteenth Amendment to the United States Constitution. Although the Supreme Court acknowledged that entry of the nolle prosequi with leave did not permanently discharge the indictment, it nevertheless affirmed. Its opinion concludes:

> Without question a defendant has the right to a speedy trial, if there is to be a trial. However, we do not understand the defendant has the right to compel the State to prosecute him if the state's prosecutor, in his discretion and with the court's approval, elects to take a nolle prosequi. In this case one jury seems to have been unable to agree. The solicitor may have concluded that another go at it would not be worth the time and expense of another effort.
>
> In this case the solicitor and the court, in entering the nolle prosequi with leave followed the customary procedure in such cases. Their discretion is not reviewable under the facts disclosed by this record. The order is affirmed.

The North Carolina Supreme Court's conclusion—that the right to a speedy trial does not afford affirmative protection against an unjustified postponement of trial for an accused discharged from custody—has been explicitly rejected by every other state court which has considered the question. That conclusion has also been implicitly rejected by the numerous courts which have held that a nolle prossed indictment may not be reinstated at a subsequent term.

A Fundamental Right

We, too, believe that the position taken by the court below was erroneous. The petitioner is not relieved of the limitations placed upon his liberty by this prosecution merely because its suspension permits him to go "whithersoever he will." The pendency of the indictment may subject him to public scorn and deprive him of employment, and almost certainly will force curtailment of his speech, associations and participation in unpopular causes. By indefinitely prolonging this oppression, as well as the "anxiety and concern accompanying public accusation," [*United States v. Ewell* (1966)] the criminal procedure condoned in this case by the Supreme Court of North Carolina clearly denies the petitioner the right to a speedy trial which we hold is guaranteed to him by the Sixth Amendment of the Constitution of the United States.

While there has been a difference of opinion as to what provisions of this Amendment to the Constitution apply to the States through the Fourteenth Amendment, that question has been settled as to some of them in the recent cases of *Gideon v. Wainwright* (1963), and *Pointer v. Texas* (1965). In the latter case, which dealt with the confrontation-of-witnesses provision, we said:

> In the light of *Gideon, Malloy,* and other cases cited in those opinions holding various provisions of the Bill of Rights applicable to the States by virtue of the Fourteenth Amendment, the statements made in *West* and similar cases generally declaring that the Sixth Amendment does not apply to the States can no longer be regarded as the law. We hold that petitioner was entitled to be tried in accordance with the protection of the confrontation guarantee of the Sixth Amendment, and that that guarantee, like the right against compelled self-incrimination, is to be enforced against the

States under the Fourteenth Amendment according to the same standards that protect those personal rights against federal encroachment. [*Malloy v. Hogan*]

We hold that the right to a speedy trial is as fundamental as any of the rights secured by the Sixth Amendment. That right has its roots at the very foundation of our English law heritage. Its first articulation in modern jurisprudence appears to have been made in Magna Carta (1215), wherein it was written, "We will sell to no man, we will not deny or defer to any man either justice or right"; but evidence of recognition of the right to speedy justice in even earlier times is found in the Assize of Clarendon (1166). By the late thirteenth century, justices, armed with commissions of gaol [British variant of *jail*] delivery and/or oyer and terminer [commissions authorizing a British judge to hear and determine] were visiting the countryside three times a year. These justices, Sir Edward Coke [English legal commentator (1552–1634)] wrote in Part II of his *Institutes*, "have not suffered the prisoner to be long detained, but at their next coming have given the prisoner full and speedy justice, . . . without detaining him long in prison." To Coke, prolonged detention without trial would have been contrary to the law and custom of England; but he also believed that the delay in trial, by itself, would be an improper denial of justice. In

The Magna Carta, signed in 1215, was the first articulation of the right to a speedy trial.

his explication of Chapter 29 of the Magna Carta, he wrote that the words "We will sell to no man, we will not deny or defer to any man either justice or right" had the following effect:

> And therefore, every subject of this realme, for injury done to him in bonis, terris, vel persona, by any other subject, be he ecclesiasticall, or temporall, free, or bond, man, or woman, old, or young, or be he outlawed, excommunicated, or any other without exception, may take his remedy by the course of the law, and have justice, and right for the injury done to him, freely without sale, fully without any denial, and speedily without delay.

Coke's *Institutes* were read in the American Colonies by virtually every student of the law. Indeed, Thomas Jefferson wrote that at the time he studied law (1762–1767), "Coke Lyttleton was the universal elementary book of law students." And to John Rutledge of South Carolina, the *Institutes* seemed "to be almost the foundation of our law." To Coke, in turn, Magna Carta was one of the fundamental bases of English liberty. Thus, it is not surprising that when George Mason drafted the first of the colonial bills of rights, he set forth a principle of Magna Carta, using phraseology similar to that of Coke's explication: "[I]n all capital or criminal prosecutions," the Virginia Declaration of Rights of 1776 provided, "a man hath a right . . . to a speedy trial. . . ." That this right was considered fundamental at this early period in our history is evidenced by its guarantee in the constitutions of several of the States of the new nation, as well as by its prominent position in the Sixth Amendment. Today, each of the 50 States guarantees the right to a speedy trial to its citizens.

The history of the right to a speedy trial and its reception in this country clearly establish that it is one of the most basic rights preserved by our Constitution.

The Right to Trial by a Local Jury

Steven A. Engel

In this article, Steven A. Engel, a law clerk to Judge Kozinski of the Ninth Circuit Court of Appeals, traces the historic importance of the "vicinage presumption" in the right to be tried by a jury of peers drawn from the district in which the accused lives. While modern courts seek jurors who are wholly unfamiliar with the crime, historically the law welcomed jurors from the neighborhood who were familiar with the accused and the crime prior to trial. England's efforts to curtail that right in the American colonies became a recurring theme in America's struggle for independence from England.

The vicinage [neighborhood or local district] presumption is as longstanding as the notion of the jury itself. In fact, local juries predate impartial ones by several centuries. The first juries were administrative bodies summoned by royal officials to provide information about their locality. The jurors represented the community in its dealings with royal officials, and it was their familiarity with local affairs that first led them to take on a judicial role. Jurors were impartial in the sense that they could not be related to either of the parties or have a financial interest in the trial, yet the law welcomed their extra-judicial knowledge of the facts of the case. If they were not familiar with the events, they were expected to investigate matters themselves prior to the trial. In the early days of the common law, the court relied more upon the jurors' commitment to their solemn oaths than it did upon the evidence presented at the trial. Indeed, it was only in the

Steven A. Engel, "1658 The Public's Vicinage Right: A Constitutional Argument," *New York University Law Review,* December 2000. Copyright © 2000 by *New York University Law Review.* Reproduced by permission seventeenth century that English law recognized defendants' right to present evidence in their defense. At a time when the law relied upon out-of-court knowledge, local juries were a functional necessity. . . .

The Framing of the Sixth Amendment

The generation that ratified the Constitution and the Bill of Rights recognized the vicinage presumption as an essential part of the right to trial by jury. In the struggle for independence, the colonists stood ready to defend "the inestimable Privilege of being tried by a Jury from the Vicinage" [Virginia Resolves (May 16, 1769)]. The colonists inveighed against the British for abridging the vicinage right by taking defendants away to England for trial and by protecting British soldiers from the justice of colonial juries. A majority of the early state constitutions expressly protected the vicinage right, and the Antifederalists criticized the federal Constitution for failing to do so adequately. The First Congress framed the Sixth Amendment with an understanding that the traditional vicinage presumption protected the structural interests of the jury system, as well as the rights of the defendant.

Although it may surprise modern eyes, the vicinage right was a recurring theme in the struggle for independence. Parliament first threatened the right in 1769, in response to Boston patriots' spirited resistance to the Stamp Act and Townshend Duties. Parliament recommended that the King revive a 1543 statute that granted the Crown the authority to try in England cases of treason committed outside the realm. That statute, enacted prior to England's colonial period, permitted the trial of treason planned and committed beyond the jurisdiction of any English courts. Parliament suggested that it could be employed to try American patriots before juries more friendly to the Crown. To the Americans, however, such an act denied them their rights as Englishmen. The Virginia House of Burgesses immediately responded to Parliament's resolution, enacting its own resolution decrying the action. Given the availability of colonial courts and juries, seizing Americans was a "new, unusual, . . . unconstitutional and illegal Mode" [as stated by the Virginia House of Burgesses] that would deprive the defendant of his right to be tried by his neighbors, as well as, in practice, his right to call witnesses in his defense. These Virginia Resolves, as they became known in the colonies, were promptly approved by the legislatures of the other American colonies.

The Impact of the Boston Massacre

The American colonists knew that the vicinage presumption protected the community's interest in law enforcement as well as the defendant's right to a fair trial. The Boston Massacre, the notorious clash between English troops and colonists that left five Bostonians dead, led to the most widely publicized trial of the revolutionary period. A distant ancestor of the [Rodney] King and [Amidou] Diallo trials, the Massacre trials involved the prosecution of unpopular law enforcement officers for the allegedly unprovoked assaults on the townspeople.

The British officers and soldiers involved in the Boston Massacre (pictured) were tried in Boston. Later trials for similar offenses were moved to a nearby province or to England.

The shootings occurred amidst increasing friction between the British garrison and Bostonians, and the case, to put it mildly, was as much a political affair as a judicial one. As one historian [Helen B. Zobel] observed, "radicals and Tories alike immediately realized the incident's tremendous propaganda value." Sam Adams and the Sons of Liberty staged numerous protests in the streets and before the town council. Paul Revere cast a best-selling print of the massacre, grossly exaggerating the incident by depicting soldiers firing wantonly into a peaceful crowd. The press was filled with highly prejudicial accounts of the incident, including a widely read pamphlet that included an appendix with ninety-six affidavits from townspeople filled with prejudicial and inadmissible evidence. The pamphlet alleged that the Massacre had resulted, not from a spontaneous disturbance, but from a planned conspiracy between the British garrison and the Customs House. These deliberate efforts to raise public passion in an already politically charged trial dwarfed the community protests that preceded the King and Diallo trials.

In contrast to those modern-day trials, however, the British officers were tried in the city in which the riots took place. The colonial justice system was not insensitive to the dangers that community prejudice posed to the defendants. The court employed its power to ensure that the Boston jury would be impartial, yet no motion was made to take the trial out of the hands of the vicinage. Indeed, such a measure well might have resulted in mob violence against the indicted soldiers. . . . The jury ultimately acquitted the captain. Similar efforts were made to secure an impartial jury in the subsequent trial of the soldiers, and the jury acquitted six of these men while finding two guilty of manslaughter. . . .

Britain Decides to Remove the Trials of Its Soldiers

Although the Americans accepted the verdicts in the Boston Massacre trials, Parliament decided not to take any more chances with the people of Boston. After the Boston Tea Party, it enacted the Act for the Impartial Administration of Justice, one of the so-called Intolerable Acts, which provided that English soldiers charged with murdering colonists while repressing civil unrest or enforcing the revenue laws would be tried outside of Boston in a nearby province or in England. Colonists denounced the Act as the "Murderer's Act," charging it with violating the English constitution and threatening the safety of the people of Massachusetts. . . .

Amidst this revolutionary climate, the vicinage right was on the agenda of the first meeting of the Continental Congress. The Congress expressed its concern with trying both American patriots and English soldiers across the seas in England. The Congress's first series of resolutions echoed the Virginia Resolves in stating that the colonies were entitled to "the great and inestimable privilege of being tried by their peers of the vicinage, according to the course of that law." The Congress also charged that the Administration of Justice Act deprived the colonists of their "rights" as Englishmen, including the right to sit in judgment on the jury. In an address to the Province of Quebec enumerating the rights of Englishmen, the Congress conveyed its belief that the vicinage presumption was inseparable from the trial by jury:

> [The] great right . . . of trial by jury . . . provides, that neither life, liberty nor property, can be taken from the possessor, until twelve of his unexceptionable countrymen and peers of his vicinage, who from that neighbourhood may reasonably be supposed to be acquainted with his character, and the characters of the witnesses, upon a fair trial, and full enquiry, face to face, in open Court, before as many of the people as chuse to attend, shall pass their sentence upon oath against him. . . .

The Declaration of Independence and Early Constitutions

The Declaration of Independence reflected these sentiments and so listed among its grievances violations of both the community and the defendant's vicinage right. The Declaration attacked the King for his approval of the Administration of Justice Act. It described such an act "of pretended Legislation" as a measure "foreign to our Constitutions" that protected the

King's armed troops "by a mock Trial, from Punishment for any Murders which they should commit on the Inhabitants of these States." The document also criticized the King's support for parliamentary acts that violated the defendant's vicinage right, "transporting us beyond Seas to be tried for pretended Offences.". . .

In the wake of the Declaration of Independence, many of the state constitutions expressly incorporated the vicinage right. The various formulas by which the constitutions guaranteed that right reflected the multiple purposes that it served. Two states required that criminal trials be held in the county in which the offense was committed. Two others declared that trial near the location of the crime was essential in order to have a proper determination of the facts. Two expressly guaranteed the defendant the right to trial by the vicinage or the "country." Although the others did not contain an express vicinage guarantee, they secured the trial by jury, which well may have been seen as implicitly protecting the vicinage. Two of these states, New York and Rhode Island, demonstrated this understanding by ratifying the federal Constitution under the assumption that the guarantee of trial by jury implied a vicinage limitation.

The text of the U.S. Constitution contained only a limited recognition of the vicinage presumption. Article III, Section 2, provided that "[t]he Trial of all Crimes, except in Cases of Impeachment, shall be by Jury; and such Trial shall be held in the State where the said Crimes shall have been committed. . . ." There was little debate on this provision, yet it clearly addressed Great Britain's primary abuse of the vicinage presumption: the transporting of American patriots to England for trial. . . .

The limited protection that the Constitution granted to the vicinage presumption was one of the Antifederalists' primary concerns with Article III. Although Article III guaranteed a trial in the state, it did not ensure that the members of the local community would sit on the jury. Patrick Henry, in the Virginia Convention, argued that to leave the vicinage right unguarded was to sacrifice the jury right itself: "Juries from the vicinage being not secured, this right is in reality sacrificed." Other Antifederalists, such as Stephen Holmes of Massachusetts, criticized the Constitution for failing to provide the defendant with the "right to insist on a trial in the vicinity where the fact was committed." As a result of these objections, a number of the state ratification conventions called for the vicinage right to be added as part of the Bill of Rights.

Given the public interest in a Bill of Rights, James Madison proposed amendments to the Constitution in June 1789. Madison's original plan was to provide a list of amendments to the text of the Constitution, rather than to add to the document a supplemental set of limitations. The original proposal contained two articles relating to the judiciary. The first provided for the rights of the accused in a criminal prosecution. Madison sought to place those rights in Article I, Section 9, as a limitation upon the power of Congress. The second provision would amend the structural provisions of Article III, Section 2, clause 3, to expand upon the original meaning of the guarantee that all trials would be by jury. Madison placed in the second structural provision the guarantee that all trials would be "by an impartial jury of freeholders of the vicinage." The text contained an exception to the vicinage presumption for cases in which the county was under enemy occupation or in general insurrection. Thus, Madison's original proposal recognized that the vicinage presumption was part of the structure of the judicial branch, not simply a right of the individual defendant. . . .

The final text altered the vicinage right so as to phrase it as a personal right of the accused, rather than as a structural provision. There does not appear to be any firm evidence of why this happened, and nothing in Madison's letters suggests that the changes responded to concern over the public's vicinage right. The structural language reflected the dominant common law tradition that viewed the vicinage presumption as a part of the trial by jury that protected both the defendant and the community. Given the Founders' widespread recognition that in all criminal trials jurors would be drawn from the vicinage, there is no evidence that the Founders believed that the change in language would weaken the structural presumption.

The Right to Counsel

Alfredo Garcia

In the following excerpt Alfredo Garcia, a professor of criminal law at St. Thomas University School of Law and author of books on the Fifth and Sixth Amendments, traces the history of the right to counsel from colonial times to the landmark Supreme Court decision *Gideon v. Wainwright* (1963). The courts in both England and America were slow in recognizing the fundamental importance of this pervasive right. However, in *Gideon* the Supreme Court stated that every person accused of a crime had a right to counsel and, if he or she could not afford it, counsel must be provided to him or her. It has become one of the most popular cases ever handed down by the Supreme Court because it provides counsel to every person accused of a crime, regardless of how poor he or she is.

The history of the right to counsel is inextricably tied to the English and colonial jurisprudence which led to the genesis of the Sixth Amendment. In examining the historical background, it is evident that the right to counsel did not receive favorable treatment in either English or early colonial jurisprudence. Instead, the right was ultimately accepted, especially in the colonies, as a response to political exigencies. England's grudging recognition of the right to counsel is betrayed by the fact that defendants accused of felonies other than treason were not entitled to lawyers until 1836.

The antipathy the British common law displayed toward the assistance of counsel derived from the government's weakness vis-a-vis its enemies. A historian of British law [W. Holdsworth] noted that the public approved of this refusal to extend the help of counsel to the accused "because the gov-

Alfredo Garcia, "The Right to Counsel Under Siege: Requiem for an Endangered Right," *American Criminal Law Review,* Fall 1991. Copyright © 1991 by the Georgetown University Law Center. Reproduced by permission of the publisher, *Georgetown Law Journal.*

ernment was so weak and its enemies so strong that it was felt, not without reason, that it must take every advantage of its enemies."

The Revolution of 1688, however, led to a more stable political situation and thus to the extension of the help of counsel to defendants accused of treason. The Treason Act of 1695 ushered a series of reforms in English criminal procedure that granted accused persons the right to notice and to compulsory process. Despite the progress brought about by these revisions, the right to counsel was extended only to defendants charged with misdemeanors or treason.

Given the English system's hostility toward counsel, it was inevitable that such distrust would be carried over to the colonies. To the extent British criminal procedure was riddled with abuse of power, the "professional" lawyer became a symbol of oppression in both England and the colonies. This aversion to the profession is manifest in the West New Jersey Charter of Fundamental Laws of 1676, which gave litigants the right to defend their cases and, concomitantly, freed them of the compulsion to hire counsel.

Eventually, a shift in this antilawyer attitude occurred in the American colonies. Unlike in England, the colonies employed the inquisitorial institution of the public prosecutor. The prosecutor wielded great power due to his familiarity with procedural niceties, the "idiosyncrasies of juries," and "the personnel of the court" [as stated by Francis Heller]. As a consequence, the assistance of counsel and the allied rights ultimately enumerated in the Sixth Amendment became essential to counter the prosecutor's advantage. Ultimately, the denial of these rights formed part of the grievances listed in the Declaration of Independence.

The right to counsel, therefore, found its way into most state constitutions after the colonies declared their independence. The assistance of counsel, in turn, complemented the correlative right to self-representation. Opposition to the Federal Constitution arose in part because the procedural protections accorded the accused in state constitutions, with the exception of the jury trial, were conspicuously missing from the new document. The adoption and passage of the Bill

of Rights, which included the trial-related safeguards outlined in the Sixth Amendment, allayed the antagonism originally directed at the Constitution.

The historical record reveals the extent to which the need
for an equilibrium of forces between the prosecution and the
accused animated the forging of the Sixth Amendment's protections. As one thoughtful commentator [F. Heller] remarked, the call for a Bill of Rights reflected the American
public's insistence on "the maintenance of a fair balance in
criminal trials, and to that end the protection of the rights of
the accused."

Preserving the rights of the accused, moreover, necessarily implied a repudiation of the English proscription of counsel in serious criminal cases.

Although the American safeguards designed to redress the
imbalance of power that existed in English procedure included the right of the accused "to have the Assistance of
counsel for his defense," the Sixth Amendment did not em-
brace the right to appointed counsel. Rather, at the time of its
enactment, the amendment connoted that "the right to counsel meant the right to retain counsel of one's own choice and
at one's expense" [as stated by William Merritt Beanex].
Nearly two centuries later, the Supreme Court took into account the transformation of American jurisprudence and pro-
gressively implied the right to appointed counsel as essential
to the structure of the Sixth Amendment. The logical culmi-
nation of this interpretation was the [Chief Justice Earl] Warren Court's landmark ruling in *Gideon v. Wainwright*, in
which the Court held that a defendant has a Sixth Amendment right to appointed counsel in state court. It is important
to scrutinize this jurisprudential development as a means of
distilling the "modern" meaning of the right to counsel.

Powell v. Alabama

The emergence of an expansive approach toward the right to
counsel may be traced to the Supreme Court's seminal decision in *Powell v. Alabama*. In *Powell*, the Court determined
that the assistance of counsel was "fundamental" in nature,
and hence essential to ensure a defendant a fair trial. The

Powell Court decided that the right comprehends "effective" assistance, rather than the mere perfunctory appearance of counsel. The majority concluded that the Due Process Clause of the Fourteenth Amendment requires the appointment of counsel in capital cases. Even though *Powell* was carefully circumscribed to its facts, it contained the seeds of a fundamental metamorphosis in the Court's conception of an attorney's role in a criminal proceeding. Implicit in this new understanding was the notion that the criminal process should strive for a modicum of equity by affording both sides the opportunity of vigorously asserting their positions.

In *Powell*, the Court expanded the scope of the Sixth Amendment by going beyond the original intent of the right to counsel clause. The clause contemplated the defendant's right to choose private counsel; it did not envision the provision of appointed counsel. The *Powell* Court recognized that a "defendant should be afforded a fair opportunity to secure counsel of his own choice." Whether counsel is appointed or selected, however, is not the sole calculus in assessing the right to counsel. The right necessarily implicates an "effective," "zealous" advocate rather than the mere "pro forma," passive appearance of a defense attorney.

Powell's factual predicate illustrates the Court's concern for effective advocacy as integral to the assistance of counsel. In that case, the famous "Scottsboro" black defendants were charged with raping two white women. The nine youthful defendants' cases were severed and three separate arraignments and trials were conducted in a single day. More important, counsel appointed to represent the "boys" were ill-prepared to represent them and their appearance amounted to a sham. Given the emotionally charged atmosphere in which the trial occurred, a lack of effective counsel inevitably ensured a conviction.

It is within this framework that *Powell* must be viewed. The majority not only abhorred the sham nature of the proceedings, but also condemned the trial court for preventing the defendants from consulting with counsel and preparing their defenses. The egregious circumstances out of which *Powell* arose led the Court to reaffirm the "fundamental character" of the right to counsel. In an oft-quoted passage, the *Powell* Court acknowledged that counsel is indispensable to the balance of power required in an adversary system of adjudication, especially when the individual does not have the means to hire an attorney. The majority wrote:

> [T]he right to be heard would be, in many cases, of little avail if it did not comprehend the right to be heard by counsel. Even the intelligent and educated layman has small and sometimes no skill in the science of law. If charged with a crime, he is incapable, generally, of determining for himself whether the indictment is good or bad. He is unfamiliar with the rules of evidence. Left without the aid of counsel, he may be put to trial without a proper charge, and convicted upon incompetent evidence, or evidence irrelevant to the issue or otherwise inadmissible. . . . He requires the hand of counsel at every step of the proceedings against him. . . . If that be true of men of intelligence, how much more true is it of the ignorant or illiterate, or those of feeble intellect.

A "logical corollary" of this rationale is that the "right to be heard" by counsel implies "the right to have counsel appointed." Although the *Powell* Court narrowly crafted its holding to apply solely to the factual circumstances of the case, it foreshadowed a broader application of its holding by emphasizing the widespread acceptance of appointed counsel in all criminal prosecutions by most states. . . .

Gideon v. Wainwright

Gideon [*v. Wainwright*] affirmed the fundamental nature of the right to counsel. Endorsing the essential character of the right, a unanimous Court adhered to the rationale underlying *Powell*. . . . The opinion acknowledged the consequences of not affording an indigent defendant counsel: an "unequal" contest in which the defendant's interests are slighted. Such a proceeding is antithetical to the values and policies upon which the adversary system is based.

Accordingly, the underpinning of *Gideon* rests on the notion that a fair trial requires a certain balance of power between the prosecution and the defense. To the extent that the government has and spends the resources necessary to secure a conviction, so must the defendant have a lawyer to combat the prosecution. Because "there are few defendants charged with a crime . . . who fail to hire the best lawyers they can get to prepare their defenses," equal protection dictates that an indigent defendant should have the assistance of counsel.

Few decisions have evoked as much popular support as *Gideon*. Indeed, Professor [Yale] Kamisar characterized *Gideon* as "one of the most popular decisions ever handed down by the United States Supreme Court." *Gideon*'s popularity is attributable to its simplicity and its common sense. As [Anthony Lewis and Abe Krash have] remarked, it is a landmark opinion because "it affirmed a right that is now fundamentally accepted in our society." Furthermore, the decision provided legitimacy to a system founded on an adversarial clash between two relatively equal sides whose conflicting interests allegedly produced an accurate result. . . . The legitimacy of the criminal adversary process, on which the accused's liberty hinges, demanded such an outcome.

CHAPTER TWO

Balancing the Right to a Fair Trial Against the Interests of Society

The Bill of Rights

The Public Does Not Have the Right to Attend Criminal Trials

Potter Stewart

In 1976 two men accused of a sensational murder in New York State requested that the public and press be barred from the hearing on their motion to suppress evidence, including confessions, which they argued should not be introduced at trial. The motion was granted, and the press was barred from the hearing and denied access to the transcript of the hearing. A newspaper reporter appealed the decision, and the case eventually reached the Supreme Court. The following selection, by Associate Justice Potter Stewart, is excerpted from the majority opinion in the case. Stewart held that the interest of the press and the public was outweighed by the defendant's right to a fair trial and neither the press nor the public had a right to attend a trial over the objection of the defendant. Stewart served on the Court from 1958 to 1981.

At a pretrial hearing on a motion to suppress allegedly involuntary confessions and certain physical evidence, respondents Greathouse and Jones, who were defendants in a state prosecution for second-degree murder, robbery, and grand larceny, requested that the public and the press be excluded from the hearing, arguing that the unabated buildup of adverse publicity had jeopardized their ability to receive a fair trial. The District Attorney did not oppose the motion and a reporter employed by petitioner, whose newspapers had given extensive coverage of the crime through the defendants' indictment and arraignment, made no objection at the

Potter Stewart, majority opinion, *Gannett Co. v. DePasquale,* 1979.

Justice Potter Stewart (pictured) held that a defendant's right to a fair trial superseded the press's and the public's access to the trial.

time of the closure motion though she was present in the courtroom. Respondent trial judge granted the motion, and, in response to the reporter's letter on the next day asserting a right to cover the hearing and requesting access to the transcript, stated that the suppression hearing had concluded and that any decision on immediate release of the transcript had been reserved. Petitioner then moved to have the closure order set aside but the trial judge, after a hearing, refused to vacate the order or grant petitioner immediate access to the transcript, ruling that the interest of the press and the public was outweighed by the defendants' right to a fair trial. . . .

The question presented in this case is whether members of the public have an independent constitutional right to insist upon access to a pretrial judicial proceeding, even though the accused, the prosecutor, and the trial judge all have agreed to the closure of that proceeding in order to assure a fair trial. . . .

This Court has long recognized that adverse publicity can endanger the ability of a defendant to receive a fair trial. . . . To safeguard the due process rights of the accused, a trial judge has an affirmative constitutional duty to minimize the effects of prejudicial pretrial publicity. . . . And because of the Constitution's pervasive concern for these due process rights, a trial judge may surely take protective measures even when they are not strictly and inescapably necessary.

Publicity concerning pretrial suppression hearings such as the one involved in the present case poses special risks of unfairness. The whole purpose of such hearings is to screen out unreliable or illegally obtained evidence and insure that this evidence does not become known to the jury. . . . Publicity concerning the proceedings at a pretrial hearing, however, could influence public opinion against a defendant and inform potential jurors of inculpatory information wholly inadmissible at the actual trial.

The danger of publicity concerning pretrial suppression hearings is particularly acute, because it may be difficult to measure with any degree of certainty the effects of such publicity on the fairness of the trial. After the commencement of the trial itself, inadmissible prejudicial information about a defendant can be kept from a jury by a variety of means. When such information is publicized during a pretrial proceeding, however, it may never be altogether kept from potential jurors. Closure of pretrial proceedings is often one of the most effective methods that a trial judge can employ to attempt to insure that the fairness of a trial will not be jeopardized by the dissemination of such information throughout the community before the trial itself has even begun. . . .

The Sixth Amendment, applicable to the States through the Fourteenth, surrounds a criminal trial with guarantees such as the rights to notice[1], confrontation[2], and compulsory process[3] that have as their overriding purpose the protection of the accused from prosecutorial and judicial abuses. Among the guarantees that the Amendment provides to a person charged with the commission of a criminal offense, and to him alone, is the "right to a speedy and public trial, by an impartial jury." The Constitution nowhere mentions any right of

---

1. to be informed of the nature of the accusations
2. the right to challenge witnesses
3. the right to obtain witnesses in one's favor

access to a criminal trial on the part of the public; its guarantee, like the others enumerated, is personal to the accused. . . .

A Safeguard Against Persecution

Our cases have uniformly recognized the public-trial guarantee as one created for the benefit of the defendant. . . . This Court held that the secrecy of a criminal contempt trial violated the accused's right to a public trial under the Fourteenth Amendment. The right to a public trial, the Court stated, "has always been recognized as a safeguard against any attempt to employ our courts as instruments of persecution. The knowledge that every criminal trial is subject to contemporaneous review in the forum of public opinion is an effective restraint on possible abuse of judicial power." In an explanatory footnote, the Court stated that the public-trial guarantee

> "is for the protection of all persons accused of crime—
> the innocently accused, that they may not become the
> victim of an unjust prosecution, as well as the guilty,
> that they may be awarded a fair trial—that one rule [as
> to public trials] must be observed and applied to all."
> Frequently quoted is the statement in 1. Cooley, *Constitutional Limitations*: "The requirement of a public trial
> is for the benefit of the accused; that the public may see
> he is fairly dealt with and not unjustly condemned, and
> that the presence of interested spectators may keep his
> triers keenly alive to a sense of their responsibility and
> to the importance of their functions. . . ."

Similarly, in *Estes v. Texas* [1965], the Court held that a defendant was deprived of his right to due process of law under the Fourteenth Amendment by the televising and broadcasting of his trial. In rejecting the claim that the media representatives had a constitutional right to televise the trial, the Court stated that "[t]he purpose of the requirement of a public trial was to guarantee that the accused would be fairly dealt with and not unjustly condemned." ("Thus the right of 'public trial' is not one belonging to the public, but one belonging to the accused, and inhering in the institutional process by which justice is administered") (Harlan, J., concurring); ("[T]he public trial provision of the Sixth Amendment is a 'guarantee to an accused'. . . [and] a necessary component of an accused's right to a fair trial . . .") (Warren, C., concurring).

Thus, both the *Oliver* and *Estes* cases recognized that the constitutional guarantee of a public trial is for the benefit of the defendant. There is not the slightest suggestion in either case that there is any correlative right in members of the public to insist upon a public trial.

While the Sixth Amendment guarantees to a defendant in a criminal case the right to a public trial, it does not guarantee the right to compel a private trial. "The ability to waive a constitutional right does not ordinarily carry with it the right to insist upon the opposite of that right" [*Singer v. United States* (1965)]. But the issue here is not whether the defendant can compel a private trial. Rather, the issue is whether members of the public have an enforceable right to a public trial that can be asserted independently of the parties in the litigation.

There can be no blinking the fact that there is a strong societal interest in public trials. Openness in court proceedings may improve the quality of testimony, induce unknown witnesses to come forward with relevant testimony, cause all trial participants to perform their duties more conscientiously, and generally give the public an opportunity to observe the judicial system [*Estes v. Texas*]. But there is a strong societal interest in other constitutional guarantees extended to the accused as well. The public, for example, has a definite and concrete interest in seeing that justice is swiftly and fairly administered. Similarly, the public has an interest in having a criminal case heard by a jury, an interest distinct from the defendant's interest in being tried by a jury of his peers. . . .

The Public Has No Constitutional Right

Recognition of an independent public interest in the enforcement of Sixth Amendment guarantees is a far cry, however, from the creation of a constitutional right on the part of the public. In an adversary system of criminal justice, the public interest in the administration of justice is protected by the participants in the litigation. Thus, because of the great public interest in jury trials as the preferred mode of fact-finding in criminal cases, a defendant cannot waive a jury trial without the consent of the prosecutor and judge. . . . But if the defendant waives his right to a jury trial, and the prosecutor and the judge consent, it could hardly be seriously argued that a member of the public could demand a jury trial because of the societal interest in that mode of fact-finding. . . . Similarly, while a defendant cannot convert his right to a speedy trial into a right to compel an indefinite postponement, a member of the general public surely has no right to prevent a continuance in order to vindicate the public interest in the efficient administration of justice. In short, our adversary system of criminal justice is premised upon the proposition that the public interest is fully protected by the participants in the litigation.

In arguing that members of the general public have a constitutional right to attend a criminal trial, despite the obvious lack of support for such a right in the structure or text of the Sixth Amendment, the petitioner and amici rely on the history of the public-trial guarantee. This history, however, ultimately demonstrates no more than the existence of a common-law rule of open civil and criminal proceedings.

Not many common-law rules have been elevated to the status of constitutional rights. The provisions of our Constitution do reflect an incorporation of certain few common-law rules and a rejection of others. The common-law right to a jury trial, for example, is explicitly embodied in the Sixth and Seventh Amendments. The common-law rule that looked upon jurors as interested parties who could give evidence against a defendant was explicitly rejected by the Sixth Amendment provision that a defendant is entitled to be tried by an "impartial jury." But the vast majority of common-law rules were neither made part of the Constitution nor explicitly rejected by it.

Our judicial duty in this case is to determine whether the common-law rule of open proceedings was incorporated, rejected, or left undisturbed by the Sixth Amendment. In pursuing this inquiry, it is important to distinguish between what the Constitution permits and what it requires. It has never been suggested that by phrasing the public-trial guarantee as a right of the accused, the Framers intended to reject the common-law rule of open proceedings. There is no question that the Sixth Amendment permits and even presumes open trials as a norm. But the issue here is whether the Constitution requires that a pretrial proceeding such as this one be opened to the public, even though the participants in the litigation agree that it should be closed to protect the defendants' right to a fair trial. The history upon which the petitioner and amici rely totally fails to demonstrate that the Framers of the Sixth Amendment intended to create a constitutional right in strangers to attend a pretrial proceeding, when all that they actually did was to confer upon the accused an explicit right to demand a public trial. In conspicuous contrast with some of the early state constitutions that provided for a public right to open civil and criminal trials, the Sixth Amendment confers the right to a public trial only upon a defendant and only in a criminal case.

But even if the Sixth and Fourteenth Amendments could properly be viewed as embodying the common-law right of the public to attend criminal trials, it would not necessarily follow that the petitioner would have a right of access under the circumstances of this case. For there exists no persuasive evidence that at common law members of the public had any right to attend pretrial proceedings; indeed, there is substantial evidence to the contrary. By the time of the adoption of the Constitution, public trials were clearly associated with the protection of the defendant. And pretrial proceedings, precisely because of the same concern for a fair trial, were never characterized by the same degree of openness as were actual trials.

Under English common law, the public had no right to attend pretrial proceedings. . . .

Closed pretrial proceedings have been a familiar part of the judicial landscape in this country as well. The original *New York Field Code of Criminal Procedure* published in 1850, for example, provided that pretrial hearings should be closed to the public "upon the request of a defendant." The explanatory report made clear that this provision was designed to protect defendants from prejudicial pretrial publicity:

> If the examination must necessarily be public, the consequence may be that the testimony upon the mere preliminary examination will be spread before the community, and a state of opinion created, which, in cases of great public interest, will render it difficult to obtain an unprejudiced jury. The interests of justice require that the case of the defendant should not be prejudged, if it can be avoided; and no one can justly complain, that until he is put upon his trial, the dangers of this prejudgment are obviated.

Indeed, eight of the States that have retained all or part of the Field Code have kept the explicit provision relating to closed pretrial hearings.

For these reasons, we hold that members of the public have no constitutional right under the Sixth and Fourteenth Amendments to attend criminal trials.

Defendants Do Not Have the Right to Private Trials

Harry Blackmun

In *Gannett Co. v. DePasquale* (1979), the Supreme Court ruled that criminal defendants could waive their right to public trials and thereby bar the public and press from the courtroom. Although the majority of the Supreme Court judges supported this decision, a minority of the judges, led by Harry Blackmun, wrote a strongly worded disagreement. They carefully examined the history of the right to a public trial and found no basis for the majority holding that there exists a right to compel a private trial.

Blackmun served on the Court from 1970 to 1991. He is perhaps best remembered as the author of the 1974 *Roe v. Wade* decision legalizing abortion.

This Court confronts in this case another aspect of the recurring conflict that arises whenever a defendant in a criminal case asserts that his right to a fair trial clashes with the right of the public in general, and of the press in particular, to an open proceeding. It has considered other aspects of the problem in deciding whether publicity was sufficiently prejudicial to have deprived the defendant of a fair trial. Compare *Murphy v. Florida* (1975) with *Sheppard v. Maxwell* (1966). And recently it examined the extent to which the First and Fourteenth Amendments protect news organizations' rights to publish, free from prior restraint, information learned in open court during a pretrial suppression hearing [*Nebraska Press Assn. v. Stuart* (1976)]. But the Court has not yet addressed the precise issue raised by this case: whether

Harry Blackmun, dissenting opinion, *Gannett Co. v. DePasquale,* 1979.

Harry Blackmun

and to what extent the Constitution prohibits the States from excluding, at the request of a defendant, members of the public from such a hearing. . . .

The History of the Right to a Public Trial

The fact the Sixth Amendment casts the right to a public trial in terms of the right of the accused is not sufficient to permit the inference that the accused may compel a private proceeding simply by waiving that right. Any such right to compel a private proceeding must have some independent basis in the Sixth Amendment. In order to determine whether an independent basis exists, we should examine . . . the common-law and colonial antecedents of the public-trial provision as well as the original understanding of the Sixth Amendment. If no such basis is found, we should then turn to the function of the public trial in our system so that we may decide under what circumstances, if any, a trial court may give effect to a defendant's attempt to waive his right.

The Court, in *In re Oliver* (1948), recognized that this Nation's "accepted practice of guaranteeing a public trial to an accused has its roots in our English common law heritage." Study of that heritage reveals that the tradition of conducting the proceedings in public came about as an inescapable concomitant of trial by jury, quite unrelated to the rights of the accused, and that the practice at common law was to conduct all criminal proceedings in public.

Early Anglo-Saxon criminal proceedings were "open-air meetings of the freemen who were bound to attend them" [according to F. Pollock]. . . .

Criminal trials were by compurgation or by ordeal, and took place invariably before the assembled community, many of whom were required to attend. This Anglo-Saxon tradition of conducting a judicial proceeding "like an ill-managed public meeting" [as stated by Pollock], persisted after the Conquest, when the Norman kings introduced in England the Frankish system of conducting inquests by means of a jury. Wherever royal justice was introduced, the jury system accompanied it, and both spread rapidly throughout England in the years after 1066. The rapid spread of royal courts led to the replacement of older methods of trial, which were always public, with trial by jury with little procedural change. The jury trial "was simply substituted for [older methods], and was adapted with as little change as possible to its new position" [according to W. Holdsworth]. This substitution of royal justice for traditional law served the Crown's interests by "enlarging the king's jurisdiction and bringing well-earned profit in fines and otherwise to the king's exchequer, and the best way of promoting those ends was to develop the institution, or let it develop itself, along the lines of least resistance" [according to Pollock].

Thus, the common law from its inception was wedded to the Anglo-Saxon tradition of publicity, and the "ancient rul[e that c]ourts of justice are public." was in turn strengthened by the hegemony the royal courts soon established over the administration of justice. . . .

By the 17th century the concept of a public trial was firmly established under the common law. Indeed, there is little record, if any, of secret proceedings, criminal or civil, having occurred at any time in known English history. Apparently, not even the Court of Star Chamber, the name of which has been linked with secrecy, conducted hearings in private. . . .

In the light of this history, it is most doubtful that the tradition of publicity ever was associated with the rights of the accused. The practice of conducting the trial in public was established as a feature of English justice long before the defendant was afforded even the most rudimentary rights. For example, during the century preceding the English Civil War, the defendant was kept in secret confinement and could not prepare a defense. He was not provided with counsel either before or at the trial. He was given no prior notice of the charge or evidence against him. He probably could not call witnesses on his behalf. Even if he could, he had no means to procure their attendance. Witnesses were not necessarily confronted with the prisoner. Document originals were not required to be produced. There were no rules of evidence. The confessions of accomplices were admitted against each other and regarded as specially cogent evidence. And the defendant was compelled to submit to examination. Yet the trial itself, without exception, was public. . . .

There is no evidence that criminal trials of any sort ever were conducted in private at common law, whether at the request of the defendant or over his objection. And there is strong evidence that the public trial, which developed before other procedural rights now routinely afforded the accused, widely was perceived as serving important social interests, relating to the integrity of the trial process, that exist apart from, and conceivably in opposition to, the interests of the individual defendant. Accordingly, I find no support in the common-law antecedents of the Sixth Amendment public-trial provision for the view that the guarantee of a public trial carries with it a correlative right to compel a private proceeding.

Public Trials in America

This English common-law view of the public trial early was transplanted to the American Colonies, largely through the influence of the common-law writers whose views shaped the early American legal systems. . . . Early colonial charters reflected the view that open proceedings were an essential quality of a court of justice, and they cast the concept of a public trial in terms of a characteristic of the system of justice, rather than of a right of the accused. . . .

This practice of conducting judicial proceedings in criminal cases in public took firm hold in all the American Colonies. There is no evidence that any colonial court conducted criminal trials behind closed doors or that any recognized the right of an accused to compel a private trial. . . .

Similarly, there is no indication that the First Congress, in proposing what became the Sixth Amendment, meant to depart from the common-law practice by creating a power in an accused to compel a private proceeding. The Constitution as originally adopted, of course, did not contain a public-trial guarantee. And though several States proposed amendments to Congress along the lines of the Virginia Declaration, only New York mentioned a "public" trial. . . . But New York did not follow Virginia's language by casting the right as one belonging only to the accused; it urged rather that Congress should propose an amendment providing that the "trial should be speedy, public, and by an impartial jury. . . ."

I am thus persuaded that Congress, modeling the proposed amendment on the cognate provision in the Virginia Declaration, as many States had urged, did merely what Pennsylvania had done in 1776, namely, added the word "public" to the Virginia language without at all intending thereby to create a correlative right to compel a private proceeding. Indeed, in light of the settled practice at common law, one may also say here that "if there had been recognition of such a right, it would be difficult to understand why . . . the Sixth Amendment [was] not drafted in terms which recognized an option" [*Singer v. United States* (1965)]. And, to use the language of the Court in *Faretta v. California* (1975): "If anyone had thought that the Sixth Amendment, as drafted," departed from the common-law principle of publicity in criminal proceedings, "there would undoubtedly have been some debate or comment on the issue. But there was none." Mr. Justice Story, writing when the adoption of the Sixth Amendment was within the memory of living man, noted that "in declaring, that the accused shall enjoy the right to a speedy and public trial . . . [the Sixth Amendment] does but follow out the established course of the common law in all trials for crimes. The trial is always public."

I consequently find no evidence in the development of the public-trial concept in the American Colonies and in the adoption of the Sixth Amendment to indicate that there was any recognition in this country, any more than in England, of a right to a private proceeding or a power to compel a private trial arising out of the ability to waive the grant of a public one. I shall not indulge in a mere mechanical inference that, by phrasing the public trial as one belonging to the accused, the Framers of the Amendment must have meant the accused to have the power to dispense with publicity.

The Significance of Public Trials

I thus conclude that there is no basis in the Sixth Amendment for the suggested inference. I also find that, because there is a societal interest in the public trial that exists separately from, and at times in opposition to, the interests of the accused, . . . a court may give effect to an accused's attempt to waive his public-trial right only in certain circumstances.

The courts and the scholars of the common law perceived the public-trial tradition as one serving to protect the integrity of the trial and to guard against partiality on the part of the court. The same concerns are generally served by the public trial today. The protection against perjury which publicity provides, and the opportunity publicity offers to unknown witnesses to make themselves known, do not necessarily serve the defendant. . . . The public has an interest in having criminal prosecutions decided on truthful and complete records, and this interest, too, does not necessarily coincide with that of the accused.

Nor does the protection against judicial partiality serve only the defendant. It is true that the public-trial provision serves to protect every accused from the abuses to which secret tribunals would be prone. But the defendant himself may benefit from the partiality of a corrupt, biased, or incompetent judge. . . .

Open trials also enable the public to scrutinize the performance of police and prosecutors in the conduct of public judicial business. Trials and particularly suppression hearings typically involve questions concerning the propriety of police and government conduct that took place hidden from the public view. Any interest on the part of the prosecution in hiding police or prosecutorial misconduct or ineptitude may coincide with the defendant's desire to keep the proceedings private, with the result that the public interest is sacrificed from both sides.

Public judicial proceedings have an important educative role as well. The victim of the crime, the family of the victim, others who have suffered similarly, or others accused of like crimes, have an interest in observing the course of a prosecution. Beyond this, however, is the interest of the general public in observing the operation of the criminal justice system. Judges, prosecutors, and police officials often are elected or are subject to some control by elected officials, and a main source of information about how these officials perform is the open trial. And the manner in which criminal justice is administered in this country is in and of itself of interest to all citizens. . . .

Important in this regard, of course, is the appearance of justice. "Secret hearings—though they be scrupulously fair in reality—are suspect by nature. Public confidence cannot long be maintained where important judicial decisions are made behind closed doors and then announced in conclusive terms to the public, with the record supporting the court's decision sealed from public view" [*United States v. Cianfrani* (1978)]. The ability of the courts to administer the criminal laws depends in no small part on the confidence of the public in judicial remedies, and on respect for and acquaintance with the processes and deliberations of those courts. Anything that impairs the open nature of judicial proceedings threatens to undermine this confidence and to impede the ability of the courts to function.

Local Trials Serve the Interests of the Community

Steven A. Engel

Since Revolutionary times, American law has been understood to dictate that jurors should be drawn from the victim's community. In recent decades, however, there has been a growing trend in high-profile criminal prosecutions to grant the requests of the accused to move the trial. Steven A. Engel, law clerk to Judge Kozinski of the Ninth Circuit Court of Appeals, argues that moving a criminal trial away from the victim's community actually undermines the legitimacy of the verdict and violates Constitutional recognition that the community has the right to try its transgressors. Local jurors express the community's judgment in the verdict, permit the trial to serve as an outlet for community concern, and interpret ambiguous statutory terms in light of the common sense of the community.

Something went wrong when an Albany jury acquitted four officers who fired forty-one bullets at an unarmed man in the Bronx. The problem lay not in the verdict itself—mistaken and panicked police officers, even horribly mistaken ones, may not be criminals. Nor did the Albany jury appear particularly biased in favor of the defendants, as a similar Simi Valley jury might have been several years before in the Rodney King trial. The problem was that twelve people from Albany spoke a verdict that was not theirs to give, and not surprisingly, the people of the Bronx refused to accept the legitimacy of a foreign verdict. The move 100 miles up the Hudson River had taken the trial out of the hands of the only jury that properly could have sat in judgment of the tragic events that claimed the life of Amidou Diallo.

Again and again in notorious crimes throughout the country, criminal defendants move to change the trial venue on the ground that they cannot obtain a fair hearing before the community in which the crime was committed. The Constitution guarantees criminal defendants the right to be tried by a jury that is both impartial and drawn from the vicinity of the crime. Yet, the publicity surrounding a criminal investigation may bring these rights into conflict by filling the minds of potential jurors with prejudicial and inaccurate information in advance of the trial. Under such circumstances, criminal defendants routinely waive their right to a local trial and request a transfer to a location less tainted by pretrial publicity.

The Diallo verdict unavoidably recalls the Rodney King trial, where a California court ordered that the officers who beat King, a black motorist in Los Angeles, be tried in Simi Valley, where the residents—and therefore the jury pool—are predominantly white. Likewise, a federal court found that the men accused in the Oklahoma City bombing, Timothy McVeigh and Terry Nichols, could not be tried anywhere in the state, and so transferred the trial to Colorado. Defendants have tried unsuccessfully to change the venue in other high-profile cases, including the trials of the police officers accused of viciously assaulting Abner Louima and the terrorists who bombed the World Trade Center. And a Texas court in the small town of Jasper (population 7,000) refused to transfer the trials of the white men accused of savagely killing a black man by tying him to the back of their pickup truck. In these cases, the trial court found that the defendants were unable to overcome the strong legal presumption that trials will be held in the vicinity where the crime was committed.

Local Juries Are Necessary

The place of a criminal trial is not a matter of accident or administrative convenience. Our law always has presumed that the defendant would be tried by representatives of the vicinage—the community in which the crime was committed —because local jurors are necessary for the jury to fulfill its function in the Anglo-American justice system. There are several justifications for such a presumption. First, local jurors generally will render the most accurate verdicts. The law no longer assumes that jurors will have personal knowledge of the facts of the crime and the character of the witnesses at trial, but their familiarity with the community and its practices allows them to evaluate best the competing narratives of the prosecutor and the defendant. Second, the vicinage presumption provides a neutral venue rule that limits the government's ability to select a forum inconvenient or hostile to the defendant.

Third, the law relies upon the subjective experience of the local community to determine whether ambiguous statutory terms apply to the circumstances of the crime. By applying the law to the facts of the case, the jury shapes the content of legal norms. In the Diallo trial, for instance, the shooting of the victim was undisputed, but the defendants' criminal liability turned upon whether the officers reasonably had believed that their lives were in danger. The jurors had to interpret the meaning of "reasonable belief" in light of their commonsense understanding of the term, an intuition based on the experience and values of their community. In defining the contours of liability, the jury necessarily decides how aggressive or restrained the law enforcement officers will be in the future. The vicinage presumption thus ensures that the community that suffered the crime makes such legal judgments. By transferring the trial to another vicinage, a trial court in effect may change the governing law in the criminal proceeding.

Fourth, and perhaps most significant, the vicinage presumption fulfills the jury's democratic function by allowing the aggrieved community to participate through its representatives on the jury. Community participation injects a democratic component into the application of the laws and the outcome of the criminal trial. By stamping the community's judgment on the verdict, the local jury legitimizes both the convictions and the acquittals of criminal defendants.

This participation is essential to what the Supreme Court has described as the "community therapeutic value" of the trial, whereby the criminal trial becomes a vehicle for healing the social rupture caused by the crime. As the Diallo and King trials showed, trying the case before a foreign jury may well eviscerate the jury's role in stamping the community's judgment on a criminal case.

Community Rights Are Ignored

Although changing the venue threatens these important public interests, the prevailing legal standards do not pay any attention to the community's interests. Every American jurisdiction permits the defendant to move the court to transfer the trial on the grounds that an impartial jury may not be obtained within the immediate community. Many jurisdictions grant the prosecutor a reciprocal right to make such a request, recognizing the strong public interest in ensuring that the jury renders an accurate verdict. However, the legal rules governing these transfers focus entirely upon the danger that prejudice may pose to the accuracy of the verdict. They make no mention of the competing community interests that underlie the initial vicinage presumption. Without exception, these rules provide that when the party seeking transfer demonstrates, to an appropriate degree of likelihood, that there is danger of partiality, then the court should transfer the trial to another venue. Courts that have construed these provisions, with a few notable exceptions, likewise have done so without acknowledging the community's interests. To these courts, the primary costs of changing the venue are largely administrative. Despite the deference appellate courts pay to trial courts when reviewing jury impartiality, lower courts often have transferred the trial as a prophylactic measure, without recognizing the important interests that have been lost. By taking the community's interests out of the picture, courts may order transfers precipitously where a less drastic remedy would suffice.

The problem behind the Diallo verdict thus is structural, and will continue to recur, so long as courts fail to understand that the transfer of criminal trials is problematic on both policy and constitutional grounds. Indeed, the generation that framed the Constitution understood that the vicinage right protected interests beyond those of the defendant. The First Congress framed the Sixth Amendment's Vicinage Clause to protect the defendant's right to a fair trial, yet it did so against the longstanding presumption that the community had its own right to adjudicate crimes committed within the district. This original understanding suggests a constitutional dimension to the public's right that should be recognized by current law.

The text of the Sixth Amendment does not exhaust the constitutional principles that underlie the criminal justice system. In a series of cases beginning with *Richmond Newspapers, Inc. v. Virginia*, the Supreme Court held that there was a constitutional right of public access to criminal trials rooted not expressly in the constitutional text, but in the history and the structure of the practice. Although the Sixth Amendment guarantees the defendant the right to a public trial, the Court found that historical practice and constitutional policy supported the community's reciprocal right to keep the trial open to the public. In describing this right of access, the Court emphasized both its strong historical roots and its continuing functional justification. Finally, the Court found the right to be necessary to the enjoyment of other constitutional rights, in particular the rights of speech, assembly, and the press found in the First Amendment. The Court thus recognized that the public, through its representatives in the media, had standing to challenge the closure of a criminal proceeding. While weighty reasons might bring a court to close a portion of a criminal proceeding, the judge must demonstrate that there is no reasonable alternative to accommodate both the public's right and the overriding interest involved.

Vicinage and Public Access Rights

The same considerations that support the public's right of access to a criminal trial justify a constitutional right for the vicinage to participate in the criminal trial. The vicinage right, like the right of public access, serves interests beyond those of the criminal defendant. Like the right of public access, it has longstanding roots in our legal tradition that testify to the favorable judgment of historical experience. The right is necessary to the enjoyment of other constitutional provisions—namely the cross-section requirement of the Sixth Amendment and the individual juror's Fourteenth Amendment right not to be excluded arbitrarily from jury service. Recognizing the right not only would ensure that courts consider the community's interests, but also would allow representatives of the affected community itself to bring claims before the court that might be ignored by the prosecution and the defense.

Just as courts may close trials to the public in extraordinary instances, they also may transfer a criminal trial in the face of weighty threats to the defendant's right to an impartial jury. However, prior to doing so, they must find first that a trial by the vicinage would prejudice the defendant's right to a fair trial in a way that a transfer might cure. The court also must hold that no reasonable alternative to transfer adequately could protect the defendant's fair trial right. In practice, such a right would require courts to try to empanel an impartial jury before concluding that a change of venue is necessary. The constitutional standard could lead in many instances to alternatives that would protect the defendant's right to a fair trial without sacrificing the interests of the community.

Although commentators debate transfer rulings in specific trials, there has been relatively little academic scrutiny of the relationship between the vicinage presumption and transfers in criminal trials. In the aftermath of the Rodney King trial, a number of scholars argued that courts must consider racial demographics in determining the appropriate venue to transfer the trial to. Should courts decide to transfer a case, it is sensible for them to try to re-create the original community, even if race is a constitutionally problematic proxy for doing so. However, virtual representation by racial or socioeconomic identity is no substitute for trying the case before the original community. Just as the American colonists could not be represented by their English cousins in Parliament, the mores and experience of one community never can be replicated elsewhere. Recognizing that Los Angeles jurors are not Simi Valley jurors, nor Albany jurors Bronx jurors, leads to the conclusion that, before transferring a case, courts first must try to solve the problem of prejudice against the defendant in the original venue.

The Right of the Accused to Confront Witnesses Is Not Absolute

Sandra Day O'Connor

The confrontation clause of the Sixth Amendment allows defendants to hear testimony and cross-examine all witnesses against them. However, society has an interest in protecting victims, especially children. Many cases of child abuse might never be brought to trial if the defendant's right to confront accusers were deemed to be absolute and children were forced to testify in the presence of their abuser. This issue came to the fore in the case of *Maryland v. Craig* (1990). The Court upheld a child abuse prosecution in which the victim testified via closed-circuit television. In the following excerpt from majority opinion, Associate Justice Sandra Day O'Connor argues that face-to-face testimony is not required in order to guarantee that a suspect's Sixth Amendment rights are protected.

O'Connor has served on the Court from 1981 to the present.

This case requires us to decide whether the Confrontation Clause[1] of the Sixth Amendment categorically prohibits a child witness in a child abuse case from testifying against a defendant at trial, outside the defendant's physical presence, by one-way closed circuit television. . . .

In March 1987, before the case went to trial, the State sought to invoke a Maryland statutory procedure that permits a judge to receive, by one-way closed circuit television, the testimony of a child witness who is alleged to be a victim

---

1. the right to confront one's accuser

Sandra Day O'Connor, majority opinion, *Maryland v. Craig*, 1990.

of child abuse. To invoke the procedure, the trial judge must first "determin[e] that testimony by the child victim in the courtroom will result in the child suffering serious emotional distress such that the child cannot reasonably communicate." Once the procedure is invoked, the child witness, prosecutor, and defense counsel withdraw to a separate room; the judge, jury, and defendant remain in the courtroom. The child witness is then examined and cross-examined in the separate room, while a video monitor records and displays the witness' testimony to those in the courtroom. During this time the witness cannot see the defendant. The defendant remains in electronic communication with defense counsel, and objections may be made and ruled on as if the witness were testifying in the courtroom.

In support of its motion invoking the one-way closed circuit television procedure, the State presented expert testimony that Brooke, as well as a number of other children who were alleged to have been sexually abused by Craig, would suffer "serious emotional distress such that [they could not] reasonably communicate" if required to testify in the courtroom. . . .

Craig objected to the use of the procedure on Confrontation Clause grounds, but the trial court rejected that contention, concluding that although the statute "take[s] away the right of the defendant to be face to face with his or her accuser," the defendant retains the "essence of the right of confrontation," including the right to observe, cross-examine, and have the jury view the demeanor of the witness. The trial court further found that, "based upon the evidence presented . . . the testimony of each of these children in a courtroom will result in each child suffering serious emotional distress . . . such that each of these children cannot reasonably communicate.". . .

We granted certiorari to resolve the important Confrontation Clause issues raised by this case.

The Confrontation Clause of the Sixth Amendment, made applicable to the States through the Fourteenth Amendment, provides: "In all criminal prosecutions, the accused shall enjoy the right . . . to be confronted with the witnesses against him."

We observed in *Coy v. Iowa* (1988) that "the Confrontation Clause guarantees the defendant a face-to-face meeting with witnesses appearing before the trier of fact." This interpretation derives not only from the literal text of the Clause, but also from our understanding of its historical roots.

We have never held, however, that the Confrontation Clause guarantees criminal defendants the *absolute* right to a face-to-face meeting with witnesses against them at trial. Indeed, in *Coy v. Iowa*, we expressly "le[ft] for another day . . . the question whether any exceptions exist" to the "irreducible literal meaning of the Clause: 'a right to *meet face-to-face* all those who appear and give evidence at trial.'". . .

Ensuring the Reliability of Evidence

The central concern of the Confrontation Clause is to ensure the reliability of the evidence against a criminal defendant by subjecting it to rigorous testing in the context of an adversary proceeding before the trier of fact. The word "confront," after all, also means a clashing of forces or ideas, thus carrying with it the notion of adversariness. As we noted in [*Mattox v. United States* (1895)] our earliest case interpreting the Clause:

> The primary object of the constitutional provision in question was to prevent depositions or *ex parte* affidavits, such as were sometimes admitted in civil cases, being used against the prisoner in lieu of a personal examination and cross-examination of the witness in which the accused has an opportunity, not only of testing the recollection and shifting the conscience of the witness, but of compelling him to stand face to face with the jury in order that they may look at him, and judge by his demeanor upon the stand and the manner in which he gives his testimony whether he is worthy of belief.

As this description indicates, the right guaranteed by the Confrontation Clause includes not only a "personal examination," but also "(1) insures that the witness will give his statements under oath, thus impressing him with the seriousness of the matter and guarding against the lie by the possibility of a penalty for perjury; (2) forces the witness to submit to cross-examination, the 'greatest legal engine ever invented for the discovery of truth'; [and] (3) permits the jury that is to decide the defendant's fate to observe the demeanor of the witness in making his statement, thus aiding the jury in assessing his credibility" [*California v. Green* (1970)].

The combined effect of these elements of confrontation—physical presence, oath, cross-examination, and observation of demeanor by the trier of fact—serves the purpose of the Confrontation Clause by ensuring that evidence admitted against an accused is reliable and subject to the rigorous adversarial testing that is the norm of Anglo-American criminal proceedings. . . .

We have recognized, for example, that face-to-face confrontation enhances the accuracy of fact finding by reducing the risk that a witness will wrongfully implicate an innocent person. [As stated in *Coy v. Iowa*,] "It is always more difficult to tell a lie about a person 'to his face' than 'behind his back.' . . . That face-to-face presence may, unfortunately, upset the truthful rape victim or abused child; but by the same token it may confound and undo the false accuser, or reveal the child coached by a malevolent adult." . . .

Giving the Accused a Full and Fair Opportunity

Although face-to-face confrontation forms "the core of the values furthered by the Confrontation Clause" [as stated in *California v. Green*], we have nevertheless recognized that it is not the *sine qua non* of the confrontation right. See *Delaware v. Fensterer* (1985) ("[T]he Confrontation Clause is generally satisfied when the defense is given a full and fair opportunity to probe and expose [testimonial] infirmities [such as forgetfulness, confusion, or evasion] through cross-examination, thereby calling to the attention of the factfinder the reasons for giving scant weight to the witness's testimony"); (oath, cross-examination, and demeanor provide "all that the Sixth Amendment demands: 'substantial compliance with the purposes behind the confrontation requirement'") (quoting *Green*).

For this reason, we have never insisted on an actual face-to-face encounter at trial in *every* instance in which testimony is admitted against a defendant. Instead, we have repeatedly held that the Clause permits, where necessary, the admission of certain hearsay statements against a defendant despite the defendant's inability to confront the declarant at trial. . . . In *Mattox* [*v. United States* (1895)], for example, we held that the testimony of a government witness at a former trial against the defendant, where the witness was fully cross-examined but had died after the first trial,

Sandra Day O'Connor

was admissible in evidence against the defendant at his second trial. We explained:

> There is doubtless reason for saying that . . . if notes of [the witness's] testimony are permitted to be read, [the defendant] is deprived of the advantage of that personal presence of the witness before the jury which the law has designed for his protection. But general rules of law of this kind, however beneficent in their operation and valuable to the accused, must occasionally give way to considerations of public policy and the necessities of the case. To say that a criminal, after having once been convicted by the testimony of a certain witness, should go scot free simply because death has closed the mouth of that witness, would be carrying his constitutional protection to an unwarrantable extent. The law in its wisdom declares that the rights of the public shall not be wholly sacrificed in order that an incidental benefit may be preserved to the accused.

. . . In sum, our precedents establish that "the Confrontation Clause reflects a *preference* for face-to-face confrontation at trial" [as stated in *Ohio v. Roberts* (1980)], a preference that "must occasionally give way to considerations of public policy and the necessities of the case" [as stated in *Mattox*]. "[W]e have attempted to harmonize the goal of the Clause—placing limits on the kind of evidence that may be received against a defendant—with a societal interest in accurate factfinding, which may require consideration of out-of-court statements" [as stated in *Bourjaily v. United States*]. We have accordingly interpreted the Confrontation Clause in a manner sensitive to its purpose and sensitive to the necessities of trial and the adversary process. . . . Thus, though we reaffirm the importance of face-to-face confrontation with witnesses appearing at trial, we cannot say that such confrontation is an indispensable element of the Sixth Amendment's guarantee of the right to confront one's accusers. Indeed, one commentator [Graham] has noted that "[i]t is all but universally assumed that there are circumstances that excuse compliance with the right of confrontation.". . .

In sum, we conclude that where necessary to protect a child witness from trauma that would be caused by testifying in the physical presence of the defendant, at least where such trauma would impair the child's ability to communicate, the Confrontation Clause does not prohibit use of a procedure that, despite the absence of face-to-face confrontation, ensures the reliability of the evidence by subjecting it to rigorous adversarial testing and thereby preserves the essence of effective confrontation. Because there is no dispute that the child witnesses in this case testified under oath, were subject to full cross-examination, and were able to be observed by the judge, jury, and defendant as they testified, we conclude that, to the extent that a proper finding of necessity has been made, the admission of such testimony would be consonant with the Confrontation Clause.

The Scope of the Accused's Right to Counsel Has Been Narrowed

Benjamin F. Diamond

In the case of *Gideon v. Wainwright* (1963), the Supreme Court held that counsel must be provided to any indigent defendant accused of a crime. Recent Court decisions have modified the *Gideon* holding by limiting the situations in which counsel must be appointed. One such case is *Texas v. Cobb* (2001). In the *Cobb* case, the defendant, Raymond Levi Cobb, confessed in the presence of appointed counsel to burglarizing a house but denied any involvement in the disappearence of the residents of the house. Several months later, without the presence of counsel, the police questioned him again about the disappearance and he confessed to murdering the residents. Cobb was convicted of the murders, but his conviction was overturned on the grounds that Cobb's lawyer had not been notified prior to Cobb's questioning, violating his Fifth Amendment right to counsel. The Supreme Court upheld the conviction, arguing that Cobb's right to counsel applied only to the burglary charge and not the murder investigation.

In the following selection legal scholar Benjamin F. Diamond contends that the Court's decision places a higher priority on controlling crime than on a defendant's right to due process and a fair trial. He concludes that the ruling could undermine the attorney-client relationship while granting greater power to the police.

Respondent [Raymond Levi Cobb] confessed to burglarizing a home but denied any involvement in the disappearance

Benjamin F. Diamond, "The Sixth Amendment: Narrowing the Scope of the Right to Counsel," *Florida Law Review*, vol. 54, 2002, pp. 1,001–1 011. Copyright © 2002 by *Florida Law Review*. Reproduced by permission.

of the Home's residents, who were reported missing shortly after the burglary. Respondent was appointed a lawyer and was released on bond. Several months later, police officers took Respondent into custody without contacting his lawyer, read him his rights pursuant to *Miranda v. Arizona*,[1] and questioned him further about the disappearances; Respondent waived his rights and confessed to the killings. A jury convicted Respondent of capital murder and sentenced him to death. The Texas Court of Criminal Appeals reversed and remanded for a new trial, reasoning that Respondent's Sixth Amendment right to counsel attached to the capital murder offense, which was "factually interwoven with the burglary," and that therefore the police were obligated to contact the lawyer and obtain his permission prior to questioning Respondent. . . .

The Court has long recognized that a defendant's Sixth Amendment right to counsel is fundamental. The purpose of this right is to protect "the unaided laymen at critical confrontations" with the government. In defining the scope of this right, the Supreme Court has struggled to balance the social interest of controlling crime with the need to protect the due process rights of the accused and the fairness of the adversarial system of justice.

In *McNeil v. Wisconsin* [1991], the Supreme Court held that the Sixth Amendment right to counsel is offense-specific. The Court cautioned that a defendant could not invoke his right to counsel once for all future prosecutions, because the right does not attach until the prosecution commences. In *McNeil*, Petitioner was arrested for armed robbery and was presented by counsel at a preliminary court appearance. Police then questioned Petitioner in a murder investigation without his lawyer present. Petitioner eventually waived his *Miranda* rights, provided the police with detailed statements, and was convicted of second degree murder and at-

---

1. Pursuant to this 1966 decision, defendants must be informed that they have the right to remain silent, that anything they say can and will be used against them in court, that they have the right to consult with a lawyer and have the lawyer present with them during interrogation, and that if they are indigent, a lawyer will be appointed to represent them without cost.

tempted first degree murder. Affirming the conviction, the Supreme Court held that while Petitioner's Sixth Amendment right to counsel had attached with respect to the armed robbery, it had not attached to the murder charge. That, the Court reasoned, was a different offense.

Creating a Different Standard

This holding stands in stark contrast to the operation of a defendant's right to counsel under the Fifth Amendment. While the Court in *McNeil* held that the right to counsel under the Sixth Amendment is offense-specific, the Court simultaneously noted that the right to counsel under the Fifth Amendment is not offense-specific. Petitioner urged the Court in *McNeil* to clarify this discrepancy and provide the police with a clear guideline—no police initiated interrogations regarding any offense if the defendant has requested a lawyer. The Court, however, declined to adopt this bright-line rule. As a result, a significant disparity exists between the right to counsel found in the Fifth Amendment and the right found in the Sixth Amendment.

In narrowing the scope of the Sixth Amendment right to counsel, the *McNeil* court was willing to approach Sixth Amendment issues with a more crime-control oriented philosophy than it had in the past. Unlike *McNeil*, earlier Sixth Amendment decisions revealed a Court more concerned about the fairness of the adversarial process and the due process rights of the accused. . . .

In the instant case [*Cobb*], however, the Court held that the Sixth Amendment right to counsel attaches only to the offense charged, and does not extend to other factually related, but uncharged crimes. The instant Court concluded that the Sixth Amendment right to counsel would extend to other uncharged crimes only if those crimes required the same proof of fact as the original, charged offense. Thus, even though the burglary and killings arose out of the same criminal transaction, Respondent's Sixth Amendment right to counsel had attached only to the burglary and not the capital murder. The police were free to interrogate Respondent about the murders without his counsel present, or without contacting his counsel prior to the questioning, and his confession was admissible at trial.

The instant Court justified its decision on two grounds. First, a defendant must still be apprised of his Fifth Amendment right to counsel prior to any custodial interrogation. In the instant case, police advised Respondent of his *Miranda* rights prior to questioning him and Respondent waived these rights. Second, the Court sought to protect society's interest in allowing the police the freedom to fully investigate unsolved crimes. To require the police to contact a defendant's lawyer prior to questioning him about the factually related offense would hamper effective law enforcement.

Dissenting Views

In a vigorous dissent, Justice [Stephen G.] Breyer, joined by Justices [John Paul] Stevens, [David] Souter and [Ruth Bader] Ginsburg, observed that the instant Court's narrow definition of offense will significantly limit the protection afforded defendants under the Sixth Amendment. The dissent noted that with a single, criminal transaction there are multiple possible "offenses" with which the defendant may eventually be charged. An armed robber, for example, that grabs the clerk and demands "your money or your life" has committed armed robbery, assault, battery, trespass, and the use of a firearm to commit a felony. The instant Court's decision allows police to interrogate the defendant charged with robbery about any of these other, uncharged offenses—the assault, the battery, the trespass—without ever having to notify his lawyer. . . .

The instant Court justified its decision, in part, on the theory that defendants are still advised of their Fifth Amendment right to counsel prior to any interrogation by police officers. But how much information do these Fifth Amendment warnings truly provide to a defendant accused of a crime? The *Miranda* warnings do not inform the accused that a lawyer is best able to negotiate a plea bargain, or that these negotiations are most effective before a defendant has submitted himself to interrogation. Nor do the *Miranda* warnings include an explanation of what charges the prosecution has brought against the defendant.

Indeed, at the heart of the instant Court's decision is the concern that requiring police officers to contact a defendant's attorney prior to questioning him about a factually related charge would undermine effective law enforcement. The instant Court's holding prevents the defense attorney from even being aware that his client is questioned, and therefore the attorney may not be able to offer his client much needed advice regarding these other offenses.

The instant Court has, therefore, potentially altered the nature of the attorney-client relationship. The attorney's relationship with his client may now be confined to only the offense charged, as other factually related charges would fall outside the scope of the lawyer's representation. This result runs counter to what a layman expects when he prepares to defend himself against a wide-ranging criminal investigation by the State. . . .

The instant Court's narrow definition of offense not only weakens a constitutional safeguard long recognized to be fundamental, but it casts potential confusion and uncertainty into the attorney-client relationship. As a result of the instant case, police have broader powers than ever before to interrogate a defendant without his attorney present. While empowering law enforcement, the instant Court has lost sight of Sixth Amendment guarantees it once considered sacrosanct.

CHAPTER THREE

Recent Controversies Regarding the Right to a Fair Trial

The Bill of Rights

Media Coverage Undermines the Fairness of Trials

Richard K. Sherwin

Richard K. Sherwin, a professor at New York Law School, analyzes the effect of the mass media on the courts. Television has created confusion between reality and fiction, fact and fantasy. Lawyers seek to exploit this confusion in order to influence the outcome of trials. For example, lawyers often use the media to control public opinion before and during trials. Sound bites, image control, and other tactics can influence the public, juries, and even judges, eroding the fairness of trials.

L et us begin with a rule of thumb. Whatever the visual mass media touch bears the mark of reality/fiction confusion. There is also a corollary to the rule: once you enter the realm of appearances it may be difficult to control how the image spins. In what follows, I offer illustrations of the rule and its corollary in the field of contemporary legal practice. Here we will encounter what has come to be known as litigation public relations. I will also trace the rule to its historic origin. This effort will lead us to the United States Supreme Court itself, the institutional source of the jurisprudence of appearances. In the course of this analysis we will see what happens to law when it comes to be dominated by image and perception. It is what happens when law enters the domain of the hyperreal, a realm in which appearances battle appearances for the sake of appearances—and where images risk spinning out of control. . . .

Richard K. Sherwin, "The Jurisprudence of Appearances: Law as Commodity," *When Law Goes Pop: The Vanishing Line Between Law and Popular Culture.* Chicago: The University of Chicago Press, 2000. Copyright © 2000 by The University of Chicago. Reproduced by permission.

A general insight about human cognition helps to account for this phenomenon. What we recognize amid the flux of events around us recapitulates what we are already capable of knowing. We are always screening out the inessential, the unfamiliar, that for which no word or category has prepared us. In this way, culture lends us eyes and ears; it teaches us to perceive, to speak, to think, and to feel. In this way we are prepared to project back into the arena of action and events (either real or simulated) the familiar forms of everyday world knowledge with which we have been provided. Order and conflict resolution, the heart and soul of law, need these cultural forms as well as a shared cognitive tool kit so that our knowledge and discourse may be adapted to the demands of specific cases. . . .

Image placement also works off another simple, but profound insight: we tend to like, and believe, what is familiar, that which makes us feel comfortable. . . .

What is significant here is the declining importance of the source of the image or the extent of its truth (if any) as compared to its power to stick in the mind. This phenomenon comports with the findings of psychologist Richard Gerrig, who has shown that it is the strength of the association between even a fictional representation and the world-knowledge it calls forth that is important. Fictional constructs like the film *Jaws* have real effects—as was made clear by the many film viewers who subsequently avoided the ocean. Similarly, if a novel or a vivid commercial or political image succeeds in evoking real feelings, or the memory of real experiences, these personal responses help to validate the image that triggered them. The more of ourselves we invest in a story, the more real it seems. Verisimilitude works best when it works off what's in our heads, in our own terms of belief. It is harder to argue with one's own feelings and memories than with someone else's. And it is precisely that sense of personal reality that helps make the evocative image seem real. Italian linguist and novelist Umberto Eco has expressed this idea in more piquant terms: "Everything looks real, and therefore it is real; in any case the fact that it seems real is real, and the thing is real even if, like *Alice in Wonderland*, it never existed." In cognitive terms we might simply say, fictional models permeate factual discourse. And law is no exception.

For a number of years now the same public relations appreciation of popular culture's "use value" that has been operating on the political front has also been at work in the domain of law. And law too is now being afflicted with some of the same problems. Chief among them are the problems that come with the conflation of truth and fiction, image and reality, fact and fantasy. We see this inside the courtroom as savvy litigators with increasing frequency emulate the popular cultural constructs and visual storytelling techniques that dominate the culture at large. But we see it outside the courtroom as well, as a growing number of lawyers deploy the strategies of public relations—using sound bites, photo ops, and a variety of spin control tactics—to win their cases in the court of public opinion. By gaining public support in a "phantom" (or virtual) trial prior to and concurrent with the real trial, prosecutors and defense attorneys seek to reap benefits inside the courtroom itself.

In order to get on the air, however, trial attorneys must package their message so that it is suitable for screening. As one trial lawyer has said, "It's a lot more interesting to a TV audience to see pictures of a genuinely weeping mother and father than a scientist or engineer saying, 'Here are the statistics with regard to [defective] pickup trucks'. . . . The parents make an indelible impression." To illustrate the point, consider the lawsuit that was triggered by the death of Cheryl Fleischner. Fleischner's husband attributed the cause of death to an anti-inflammatory drug, Voltaren, which Fleischner had been taking for a liver problem. When the story reaches CNN its opening sequence takes us to a cemetery. There's Mr. Fleischner, kneeling at his wife's gravesite. He's distraught, calling his wife's name, crying as he strokes her gravestone. Then he recounts what it was like toward the end: "She was begging—she was screaming at the top of her lungs, 'Joe, make them take it out of me!' She didn't know what it was, but what it was was her liver self-destructing." "There should have been things to prevent this from happening," he adds. It is a sentiment with which Fleischner's attorney is quick to agree: "It makes me angry that there was absolutely no knowledge of, you know, she, here she is taking it with a glass of water every day not knowing that she actually is poisoning her system."

Compelling images, real emotion, good TV—and unquestionably a good thing for the Fleischner lawsuit. Little wonder that lawyers and their clients are increasingly willing to take advantage of the media's need for this kind of dramatic programming. Like the parents of the coed who was raped and murdered in her college dormitory. Their $25 million lawsuit against both the murderer and the university gained force as the parents, with the help of their publicist, made the rounds on the TV talk-show circuit. As they grieved, and railed, unopposed, against the alleged insensitivity of the college president, millions watched—among them students, alumni, the Board of Trustees, and presumably the college president himself, not to mention prospective jurors and other potential trial participants. . . .

How Lawyers Use the Media

In short, legal spin control has come to be viewed as but another tool in the lawyer's toolbox. And like the use of visuals inside the courtroom, when one side's got it, the other side is often well advised to do the same. As one practitioner [attorney Mary Lovitz Schmidt] warned, "Sound bites can kill. They can destroy reputations, or they can communicate a positive message to a vast audience. . . . How does a lawyer meet this new challenge? Those savvy to the risks facing their client, often engage the help of a communications consultant with expertise in litigation support."

There are a number of different messages, serving different strategic purposes, that lawyers may wish to convey via the mass media. For example, federal and state prosecutors may use negative publicity prior to trial to antagonize or "demoralize" the accused, making it easier for the government to convict, or likelier that the accused will forsake trial for the benefits of plea bargaining, aided perhaps by his having cooperated with the government. One may consider in this regard the arrest, on criminal charges of inside trading, of Richard

Wigton in 1987, at the direction of then United States Attorney for the Southern District Rudolph Giuliani. Giuliani deliberately exploited the image of Wigton being dragged away in handcuffs from the trading floor before waiting television cameras. Wigton's dramatic televised arrest, together with the subsequent, and also media-coordinated, arrest of Robert Freeman in his office at the established investment banking firm Goldman, Sachs, were meant to send a clear signal to others currently under investigation—a group that included Dennis Levine, Ivan Boesky, and Michael Milken—federal prosecutor Giuliani meant business.

Under the public pressure generated by Giuliani, Milken, dismissed by his brokerage firm, Drexel Burnham Lambert, which would later be forced into bankruptcy, admitted a share of wrongdoing. Milken offered to cooperate with the government and eventually succeeded in working out a deal with Giuliani, as did Ivan Boesky, who found himself in a similar situation. The information Giuliani had fed the media, both through press conferences and via "unnamed sources," helped him to publicize and control the direction of his campaign against white-collar crime. And though some charges, like the ones against Richard Wigton and Robert Freeman, were quietly dropped later on, it hardly mattered. By that time Giuliani had already left the U.S. Attorney's office —in preparation for his run for the higher public office of mayor of New York. The dramatic images of his days as a federal prosecutor ensured that Giuliani's reputation for crime-busting would be securely imprinted in the public's mind.

The Media Mobilize Public Opinion

Aside from seeking to influence the accused, lawyers may also use the media to mobilize public opinion in the hope that pressures from that source will influence other trial participants, such as jurors, prosecutors, judges, and publicity-sensitive lawyers and witnesses in the case. For example, in the course of defending alleged Nazi war criminal John Demjanjuk, Michael Tigar followed a strategy of cultivating media attention that would reflect poorly on the prosecution's case. His goal was to disseminate the message that the power of extradition had been abused or mistakenly used against Demjanjuk. According to Tigar, the message was specifically directed at senior officials in the United States Department of Justice in the hope that they might conclude that they would be better off simply to "cut their losses" and preserve the discretionary power that they maintained rather than risk an adverse ruling in the *Demjanjuk* case that might impose additional restrictions on their field of operation. In another case, when prominent attorneys Clark Clifford and Robert Altman were prosecuted for lying to bank regulators, defense lawyers sought out the public relations services of Hill & Knowlton to fight the charges in the media. This ensured that the defendants' story would gain broad public exposure. Such efforts typically seek either to stave off indictment altogether or at least to create conditions conducive to a favorable plea agreement.

Judges may also be susceptible to this kind of influence, for they too (particularly those who are elected) are sensitive to adverse as well as laudatory publicity. Notably, the kind of influence that may be sought in this regard need not focus on a judge's ultimate ruling in the case. It may be sufficient to use an extrajudicially generated atmosphere to affect how the judge presides over the trial. A judge may affect the outcome of a case in a number of different ways: by projecting an air of skepticism (or support) toward a particular witness or attorney or evidentiary submission; by supporting (or denying) an attorney's objections concerning the admission of evidence or the examination of witnesses or the instructions the jury will receive on the law. By affecting any of these judicial functions, extrajudicial publicity can have an effect on the outcome of a trial. Litigators may also use the mass media to help ensure that judges hear their arguments in as many places as possible. . . .

Rules Against Trial by Spin

In theory, of course, there are rules against trial by spin control. According to the American Bar Association's Model Rules of Professional Conduct for lawyers, a lawyer is prohibited from making an out-of-court statement that "will have a substantial likelihood of materially influencing an adjudicative proceeding." That standard has been upheld by the Supreme Court, and a majority of the states subscribe to it. Indeed, according to the Supreme Court, "Few, if any, interests under the Constitution are more fundamental than the right to a fair trial by 'impartial jurors.'" And it is precisely this right that lawyers' "extrajudicial statements" put at risk. As the Court explained:

> The outcome of a criminal trial is to be decided by impartial jurors, who know as little as possible of the case, based on material admitted into evidence before them in a court proceeding. Extra-judicial comments on, or discussion of, evidence which might never be admitted at trial and *ex parte* statements by counsel giving their version of the facts obviously threaten to undermine this basic tenet.

Yet, as a practical matter, the operative standard ("materially influencing an adjudicative proceeding") is notoriously elusive and difficult to prove. In any event, nothing in the current legal ethical canon directly forbids lawyers from disseminating fictions outside the courtroom. Nor do they ignore the need for extrajudicial communications. For example, the model rules explicitly recognize that communications of this kind are permissible where "a reasonable lawyer would believe a public response is required in order to avoid prejudice to the lawyer's client." In a culture of adversarial justice, where competitive pressures insistently remind lawyers of the need to maintain and grow their client base, strategies that serve the client's interest are hardly likely to be disregarded. Litigation public relations has clearly become such a strategy. The rules that currently govern lawyer behavior are unlikely to stop it.

Informed Jurors Can Be Impartial

Newton N. Minow

Newton N. Minow is a lawyer, a law professor, and the former chairman of the FCC, who became famous for calling television a "vast wasteland" in 1961. In the following selection he discusses the jury selection process. Historically a jury of one's peers meant a jury of neighborhood men who knew the accused and were familiar with the crime. Contemporary thinking has reversed this concept by defining an impartial jury as an ignorant one. Unfortunately, the search for jurors uninformed about a particular case leads to the undesirable result of drawing juries from people who are generally uninformed and ignorant. Minow concludes that the legal system must accept the fact that jurors will have prior knowledge of the crimes and defendants on trial.

If, after sleeping for several hundred years, Rip van Winkle woke up today and walked into a courtroom, he would be surprised by the way we pick juries.

In 1807, when Aaron Burr was on trial for treason, Burr's lawyer said to the court, "We can't get a fair jury because there has been too much publicity. We don't want anybody who knows anything about the case."

The argument went to Chief Justice John Marshall, who said, "Well, that's impossible. We don't want to discourage citizens from being well-informed. They can be on the jury provided they say they will be fair and decide the case on what they hear in the courtroom."

Newton N. Minow, "Impartial Jurors, Impartial Juries," Markkula Center for Applied Ethics, keynote address, Markkula Center's conference, January 1997. Copyright © 1997 by Newton N. Minow. Reproduced by permission.

Through the years, we've changed that approach, but little else in the legal system is terribly different from what Rip van Winkle would have found 200 years ago.

If he stepped outside the courtroom, however, he wouldn't believe what he saw. He would discover radio, television, cable, satellites, telephones, computers, wireless communication, faxes. He would even discover the Internet. There's been a revolution outside the courtroom.

Today, most people in the United States get most of their information from radio and television rather than from print (although 64 percent of the population do read newspapers). The radio is on for most people more than three hours a day. Television is on as much as seven hours a day. We now have a media-saturated society.

So if a case involves a high-profile defendant who has become a household name—a Lt. Col. Oliver North or a Mayor Marion Barry or a Manuel Noriega or a *Valdez* Capt. Joseph Hazelwood or Leona Helmsley or Theodore Kaczynski or Mike Tyson or O.J. Simpson—how can we select jury members who have not heard of these defendants?

Megan's Law

A good illustration is Megan's Law. Megan was a 7-year-old girl who was lured into a house across the street from her home in New Jersey, sexually abused, and then murdered. The person suspected of the crime had been recently released from prison, and he had a long record of prior sexual abuse.

Aaron Burr's trial for treason in 1807 was one of the first where lawyers argued that an informed jury would be prejudiced against the defendant. The judge overruled Burr's lawyers.

The community was very upset. They went to the state legislature, and a law was passed—Megan's Law—which required the notification of neighbors in a community where a person with a record of that kind was released.

When the man charged with Megan's murder came to trial . . . , defense lawyers asked prospective jurors, "Do you know what Megan's Law is?" And if the prospective juror said yes, the defense argued, "We want that juror stricken because he or she will connect this defendant with that case. That juror will know the defendant has a criminal record, and he won't be able to have a fair trial."

The problem is that almost every person who lives in New Jersey knows what Megan's Law is. . . .

I think it's madness, in today's mass media society, to search for jurors who know nothing. We have to stop being Don Quixote, whether we're in New Jersey or somewhere else, looking for jurors who are ignorant.

Just as Chief Justice Marshall decided in 1807, we have to recognize the difference between an impartial juror and an impartial jury. The whole concept of having 12 people on a jury is to bring people of diverse backgrounds and perspectives into one room to decide a case. It is not to find 12 people who are all the same.

A Jury of Peers

The origins of the jury system are in 11th-century England. The concept was that people were entitled to a jury of their peers. At that time, a peer meant someone who knew the accused, someone who lived in the neighborhood and knew who was a liar and who would tell the truth. If the potential juror was a stranger, he could not serve on a jury. Somehow, over the centuries, we turned that upside down.

In fact, we've turned the tables. We now ask jurors more about themselves than they may learn in the courtroom about the parties in the dispute. When a person is called for jury duty, we give him or her a massive questionnaire. In some cases, the questions can go on for 100 pages.

[In 1996], a woman named Dianna Brandborg was called for jury duty in Texas and given a series of questions to answer, such as What is your income? What is your religion? What books do you read? What are your favorite television programs? Have you ever been divorced?

She finally got upset and said, "I'm entitled to some privacy. These questions are nobody's business but my own." The judge said, "OK, lady, you're going to jail for contempt," and he put her in prison.

She should have told the judge the story about the young couple who went to the zoo to see the hippopotamus. They looked at that hippopotamus from every angle for about a half-hour, whispering to each other. Finally, they went up to the zoo keeper and said, "Sir, is that a male or a female hippopotamus?" The zoo keeper answered, "That is a question that should be of interest only to another hippopotamus."

Unsullied Justice

In 1871, Mark Twain attended a trial in Virginia and witnessed the jury selection. He wrote:

> I remember one of those sorrowful farces in Virginia, which we call a jury trial. A noted desperado killed Mr. B., a good citizen, in the most wanton and cold-blooded way. Of course, the papers were full of it; all men capable of reading read about it; and, of course, all men not deaf and dumb and idiotic talked about it.

> A minister, intelligent, esteemed and well respected, a merchant of high character and known probity, a mining superintendent of intelligence and unblemished reputation, a quartz mill owner of excellent standing were all questioned in the same way, and all were set aside from the jury.

> Each said public talk and the newspaper reports had not biased his mind, but that sworn testimony would overthrow any previously formed opinion and would enable him to render a verdict without prejudice and in accordance with the facts.

> But such men could not be trusted with the case. Ignoramuses alone could mete out unsullied justice.

What would Mark Twain say about looking for jurors in New Jersey who never heard of Megan's Law? What would he say about moving the Kaczynski case from Kansas City to Denver, as if that would change what people know about the Unabomber?

We live in a world where the mass media are omnipresent. As we seek to reconcile the courts and the mass media, we ought to start by ending the practice where defendants and prosecutors know more about the jurors than the jury will ever know about the prosecutors and defendants.

Terrorism Suspects Should Be Tried by Military Tribunals

Peter J. Wallison

In November 2001, President George W. Bush issued an executive order authorizing the use of military tribunals to try suspected terrorists. Critics argued that the use of such trials, which allow for more secrecy and flexibility than domestic criminal trials, would violate suspects' right to receive a fair trial. In the following selection, Peter J. Wallison argues that military tribunals are the appropriate venue to try terror suspects. He points out that terrorists are war criminals and are therefore not entitled to the same level of protection as criminal suspects. Due to the nature of the threat that terrorists pose, Wallison contends, it is necessary to use a legal standard that places more emphasis on the protection of society than the rights of the accused. Wallison is a fellow at the American Enterprise Institute, a conservative public policy research organization. He was counsel to President Ronald Reagan.

The protests over the president's decision to authorize military tribunals to try terrorists call to mind Barry Goldwater's remark that "extremism in defense of liberty is no vice."

Stripping away the name-calling about kangaroo courts and star chambers, most of the arguments seem to be that there is only one way to conduct a trial, no matter what the offense and despite the fact that the Supreme Court in the past has not found these special tribunals to be inconsistent with the Constitution.

This inflexible approach is, in a way, as extreme as the views that condone terrorism itself, and the consequences of adopting it would ultimately help terrorism achieve its purposes.

Peter J. Wallison, "In Favor of Military Tribunals," *Christian Science Monitor*, www.csmonitor.com, January 3, 2002, p. 9. Copyright © 2002 by The Christian Science Publishing Society. All rights reserved. Reproduced by permission.

A little thought will reveal the problem the president confronts. Bringing Osama bin Laden and his henchmen to justice in a US court could require the government to reveal sensitive intelligence information, which could make it difficult to stop other terrorists. Yet without the information gained through intelligence sources, it could be impossible to convince a jury that these criminals and terrorists are guilty beyond a reasonable doubt.

More Difficult to Convict in Criminal Court

Even in revealing secret intelligence, it may not be possible to meet the standards of a US criminal court for convicting Mr. bin Laden or his co-conspirators. When the criminal justice system deals with organized crime, it is frequently unable to gain convictions without the testimony of someone who has direct knowledge of the culpability of the Mafia boss.

That's why the traditional method of reaching the top of a crime organization is to convict those lower down and work up the chain with testimony of those already convicted or in jeopardy of conviction. These witnesses can provide evidence that a person ordered a crime, even though he did not actually perform the criminal act. This doesn't always work; witnesses may not be willing to talk or there may be none. Al Capone was famously convicted only of tax evasion, when he probably ordered many murders.

The inability to convict a criminal does not mean he is innocent. We have set the standards for conviction very high, because, in balancing society's risks against the risk of punishing an innocent person, we would rather let the guilty go free than convict the innocent. That is a policy with which few in a civilized society will quarrel, but we should recognize it as striking a balance between two competing objectives.

Striking a Different Balance

Should the same balance apply to trying terrorists? To answer this, it's necessary to distinguish between criminal and terrorist acts. Although there are exceptions, almost all criminal acts injure or kill relatively few people; they are carried out for reasons that we can connect to human impulses, such as greed or anger. We have a sense, then, that such acts are relatively rare, that we can take practical steps to reduce the chances that we will be victimized, and that society's risks are to some degree limited.

Acts of terrorism, however, are more than criminal acts; they are intended to kill or injure many people, more or less at random, simply to induce fear. Under these circumstances, when confronted by terrorism we must ask whether it is still good policy to let the guilty go free for fear of punishing the innocent.

Here, it seems sensible instead to strike a different balance —one that puts greater weight on protection of society than on protection of an alleged criminal's rights. If we have evidence that a person may be responsible for ordering an act that killed thousands, it makes no sense to let him go free—so he can do it again—because we don't have sufficient evidence to convict him beyond a reasonable doubt.

Doing Justice to Terrorists and Ourselves

Thus, the issue is stark. Inflexible advocates of using the criminal courts must be willing to see some terrorists go free if there is insufficient evidence to convict. That's how our criminal justice system is intended to work, and that's the result it will inevitably produce. Those who advocate this should have the burden of demonstrating why society should be interested in striking this balance. To date, they have failed to recognize that there is a balance; they appear to believe that only the American civil jury can produce justice.

But this is surely wrong. We don't know how the terrorist trials will be conducted; trials that do not meet the standards of criminal trials are not for that reason kangaroo courts. American military officers sworn to do justice are not likely to be less fair than civil juries. It is not even clear that the trials will be wholly secret, only that the portions presenting evidence based on intelligence sources will be closed.

It has been said that the Constitution is not a suicide pact. The president's proposal shows us that, within constitutional constraints, we have the flexibility and capacity to do justice to terrorists and to ourselves.

Terrorism Suspects Should Not Be Tried by Military Tribunals

The Economist

In November 2001, U.S. president George W. Bush issued an order authorizing the use of military tribunals to try members of the terrorist group al Qaeda and other suspected terrorists. Such tribunals do not guarantee defendants the constitutional rights outlined in the Sixth Amendment. The Bush administration defended its decision to use such trials on the grounds that terrorist suspects are enemy combatants and therefore are not entitled to the same degree of constitutional protection as civilian criminal defendants. In the following selection the *Economist*, a conservative British newspaper, strongly condemns the U.S. policy. The *Economist* concludes that civilian courts can be adapted in order to treat terror suspects fairly while protecting the nation from terrorist threats.

You are taken prisoner in Afghanistan, bound and gagged, flown to the other side of the world and then imprisoned for months in solitary confinement punctuated by interrogations during which you have no legal advice. Finally, you are told what is to be your fate: a trial before a panel of military officers. Your defence lawyer will also be a military officer, and anything you say to him can be recorded. Your trial might be held in secret. You might not be told all the evidence against you. You might be sentenced to death. If you are convicted, you can appeal, but only to yet another panel of military officers. Your ultimate right of appeal is not to a judge but to politicians who have already called everyone in the prison where you are held "killers" and the "worst of the worst". Even if you are acquitted, or if your appeal against conviction succeeds, you might not go free. Instead you could be returned to your cell and held indefinitely as an "enemy combatant".

Overreaction

Sad to say, that is America's latest innovation in its war against terrorism: justice by "military commission". Overreaction to the scourge of terrorism is nothing new, even in established democracies. The British "interned" Catholics in Northern Ireland without trial: Israel still bulldozes the homes of families of suicide bombers. Given the barbarism of September 11th, it is not surprising that America should demand retribution—particularly against people caught fighting for al-Qaeda in Afghanistan.

This newspaper [the *Economist*] firmly supported George Bush's battles against the Taliban [in Afghanistan] and Saddam Hussein [in Iraq]. We also believe that in some areas, such as domestic intelligence gathering, his government should nudge the line between liberty and security towards the latter. But the military commissions the Bush administration has set up to try al-Qaeda suspects are still wrong—illiberal, unjust and likely to be counter-productive for the war against terrorism.

The day before America's Independence Day celebrations last week [July 2003], the Pentagon quietly announced that Mr Bush had identified six "enemy combatants" as eligible for trials before military commissions, which are to be set up outside America's civilian and military court systems. The Pentagon did not release the names of the accused, or any charges against them, but the families of two British prisoners and one Australian held at the American naval base at Cuba's Guantanamo Bay were told by their governments that their sons were among the six deemed eligible for trial.

The Australian government's failure to protest about this has caused protests. British ministers have expressed "strong reservations" about the commissions. In the past, they have asked for British citizens caught in Afghanistan to be sent home for trial in British courts—just as Mr Bush allowed John Walker Lindh, a (white, middle-class Californian) member of the Taliban, to be tried in American courts.

Dispensing with the Rules of Justice

American officials insist that the commissions will provide fair trials. The regulations published by the Pentagon stipulate that the accused will be considered innocent until proven guilty beyond a reasonable doubt, that he cannot be compelled to testify against himself, and that the trials should be open to the press and public if possible.

The problem is that every procedural privilege the defendant is awarded in the regulations is provisional, a gift of the panel which is judging him. The regulations explicitly deny him any enforceable rights of the sort that criminal defendants won as long ago as the Middle Ages. Moreover, the planned commissions lack the one element indispensable to any genuinely fair proceeding—an independent judiciary, both for the trial itself and for any appeal against a conviction. The military officers sitting as judges belong to a single chain of command reporting to the secretary of defence and the president, who will designate any accused for trial before the commissions and will also hear any final appeals. For years, America has rightly condemned the use of similar military courts in other countries for denying due process.

Why dispense with such basic rules of justice? Mr Bush's officials say they must balance the demand for fair trials with the need to gather intelligence to fend off further terrorist attacks. Nobody denies that fighting terrorism puts justice systems under extraordinary strain. But this dilemma has frequently been faced by others without resorting to military trials. The established procedure is to pass special anti-terrorism laws, altering trial rules somewhat to handle terrorist cases, but not abandoning established court systems, and trying to retain the basic rights of those accused as far as possible. Britain and Spain have done this. There is no reason why America's own civilian courts, which have successfully tried plenty of domestic and foreign terrorists (including Mr Lindh), could not be adapted to this purpose.

A Shadow Court System

Since the 2001 attacks, the Bush administration has avoided America's own courts repeatedly. Soon after the attacks, Mr Bush issued his executive order permitting military commissions outside the purview of the courts. Since then, his administration has imprisoned some 680 people at Guantanamo Bay precisely because it believed that the naval base, held on a perpetual lease, is outside the reach of anyone's courts, including America's. It has also claimed the right to arrest American citizens, even on American soil, as "enemy combatants" and to imprison them without charge until the war on terrorism is over. Appeals by civil libertarians to America's court system have been resisted at every stage.

Mr Bush could have asked Congress to pass new antiterrorism laws. Instead, he is setting up a shadow court system outside the reach of either Congress or America's judiciary, and answerable only to himself. Such a system is the antithesis of the rule of law which the United States was founded to uphold. In a speech on July 4th [2003], Mr Bush rightly noted that American ideals have been a beacon of hope to others around the world. In compromising those ideals in this matter, Mr Bush is not only dismaying America's friends but also blunting one of America's most powerful weapons against terrorism.

Jury Nullification: Democracy in Action or Anarchy?

Julius J. Marke

Jury nullification is a phenomenon in which a jury finds a defendant not guilty despite the defendant's obvious guilt. In most cases, by finding the defendant not guilty, the jury is protesting a law it deems unjust. In the following selection Julius J. Marke, Distinguished Research Professor of Law at St. John's University, analyzes the history of jury nullification, and cites recent examples in which juries have set guilty defendants free. Although these verdicts have undermined the public's trust in the jury system, history shows that the power of the jury to vote its conscience is actually a force for improving and perfecting the law.

Jury nullification, despite the role it played in the O.J. Simpson trial,[1] has had a long and meaningful tradition.

The Trial of William Penn

In that context, the Seventeenth Century trial of William Penn, founder of Pennsylvania, and *Bushell's Case* which arose from it, played a dramatically inspiring role.

Prior to Penn's trial, judges could require juries in criminal trials to render a verdict not only on the facts in issue, but as well on the applicable law. Questions of law involved in criminal cases, judges then maintained, were not so complicated as to excuse jurors from reaching a verdict.

1. In 1995 Simpson was found not guilty of murdering his ex-wife and her friend. During the trial, the defense had cited misconduct by the Los Angeles Police Department (LAPD) and had urged the jury to "send a message" to the LAPD by finding Simpson innocent.

Julius J. Marke, "The Intriguing Doctrine of Jury Nullification," www.freedomlaw.com, June 17, 2004. Copyright © 2004 by Julius J. Marke. Reproduced by permission of the literary estate of Julius J. Marke.

Judges used many methods to force a jury to do as they charged. A jury could be locked up, without water, food, heat, tobacco, or light, until it returned a unanimous verdict or one the judge directed. Judges could also levy a fine against members of the jury if they brought in a contrary or "corrupt" verdict and even impose imprisonment until the fine was paid.

Penn was placed on trial in the Old Bailey Court in 1670 for the crime of "tumultuous assembly," because he preached a sermon in Grace Church Street in violation of the "Conventicle Act" which prohibited any meeting for worship other than those of the Church of England. The Court ordered the jury to find Penn guilty, for if they found the Quakers had met at all, the very meeting by itself was unlawful. The jury, however, found that the meeting had taken place, but refused to find the law had been violated.

Penn, at the time, was only 26 years old, and had to conduct his own defense, as accused persons in criminal cases in those days were not allowed counsel to represent them.

The trial is a dramatic example of the cavalier methods used by judges at the time. The jury consisted of twelve ordinary middle-class men selected at random from the jury rolls of the City of London. The ten judges who heard the case included the Lord Mayor, the Recorder (a Magistrate), and other representatives of government who were motivated to enforce the "Conventicle Act."

As we read the transcript of the trial (which Penn published in 1670 as *The People's Ancient and Just Liberties, Asserted in the Trial of William Penn and William Mead. . . . Against The Most Arbitrary Procedure Of That Court*), Penn's logic and legal acumen must be admired. He baited the judges so skillfully on the role of the Common law, that they in turn tired to heckle and bully him. Finally, completely frustrated, they ordered that he be locked up in the bale dock. The bale dock was a locked cage, recessed below the floor level, located at the very end of the courtroom. There he could be heard but not seen by the jury.

When the jury returned a verdict of "guilty of speaking in Grace Church Street," the Lord Mayor shouted out, "was it not an unlawful assembly? You mean he was speaking to a tumult of people there?" The jury refused to so find.

The Recorder then angrily responded, "Gentlemen, you shall not be dismissed till you bring in a verdict which the court will accept. You shall be locked up, without meat, drink, fire and tobacco. You shall not think thus to abuse the court. We will have a verdict by the help of God or you shall starve for it."

Penn objected: "My jury, who are my judges, ought not to be thus menaced. Their verdict should be free—not forced. The agreement of twelve men is a verdict in law . . . and if, after this, the jury brings in another verdict, contrary to this, I affirm they are perjured men."

At this point while Penn was still talking, the soldiers started to push the jury back to the juryroom and then occurred one of the most inspiring incidents in the annals of English jurisprudence.

Penn called out: "Ye are Englishmen, mind your privilege, give not away your right."

And the jury replied, "Nor will we ever do it."

The jury was kept for two days and nights, without food, water, and heat, but refused to change its verdict. Finally the court ended the trial abruptly, fining each juror forty marks and committing them to imprisonment until they paid their fines.

Bushell, the foreman, and the other jurors obtained a writ of habeas corpus from the Court of Common Pleas. Releasing them from their imprisonment, Chief Justice Sir John Vaughan held: "for if it be demanded what is the fact? The judge cannot answer it: if it be asked, what is the law in this case, the jury cannot answer it." Although the judgment was later reversed on appeal because the Court of Common Pleas did not have jurisdiction in criminal matters, *Bushell's Case* established the right of trial juries to decide cases according to their convictions.

The Trial of Peter Zenger

Andrew Hamilton, one of the foremost attorneys in the Colonies, used the case with telling effect as a precedent in

Peter Zenger's trial in 1735 in New York, which established freedom of the press.

Zenger was accused of publishing a seditious libel in his newspaper defaming the Governor General of the Provence of New York. Though the Court ruled that the truth of a seditious libel could not be set up as a defense as a matter of law, Hamilton insisted, based on *Bushell's Case*, that it is for the jury to determine whether Zenger's comments were true. "The right of the jury," he argued, "to find such a verdict in their conscience do think is agreeable to their evidence, is supported by the authority of *Bushell's Case* beyond any doubt. . . ."

The jury followed his advice. and despite the judge's charge to the contrary, acquitted Zenger.

Bushell's Case gave a new meaning to the jury system in that it made the jury an equal to the executive and legislative branches of the government in the enforcement of criminal law.

In this context, it is recognized as the power of the jury to nullify the law by reflecting in their verdict the "Conscience of the Community," and is considered "one of the most potent forces in the criminal law."

Jury Nullification

As brought out by Professor A.D. Leipold, in his article "Rethinking Jury Nullification," "Nullification occurs when the defendant's guilt is clear beyond a reasonable doubt, but the jury based on its own sense of justice or fairness, decides to acquit [against the evidence, the judge's legal instructions and a legislative definition of culpable conduct]. In terms of raw power, nullification has few parallels: rarely can a public entity, make such a critical decision with no obligation to justify its action and with no recourse for the aggrieved party."

Jury nullification has been praised, in that the acquittal reflects a democratic process by which the jury can interpose its own moral or political judgment in defiance of an unpopular expression of governmental action.

By the same process, however. it has been denounced as an act of anarchy.

In addition to the Simpson Case, jury nullification has played a significant role in other recent high profile cases, in which despite the obvious evidence that the defendant committed the crime charged yet the jury disregarded the evidence and acquitted in whole or part. For example, those involving Washington, D.C., Mayor Marion Barry (although the Mayor was videotaped smoking cocaine, the jury convicted Barry of only one misdemeanor count of drug possession, acquitted on another and deadlocked on the remaining twelve charges); Dr. Jack Kevorkian (although the evidence was uncontroverted that Kevorkian had assisted in the suicide of the deceased, in violation of Michigan law, still the jury acquitted him); and Oliver North (a former White House aid, [he] was acquitted of nine of the twelve charges against him, in that he lied to Congress, obstructed justice by diverting funds in the sale of arms to Iran and money to the Nicaraguan Contra rebels; despite the judge's charge that his claim that he acted on the orders of superiors was not a defense, . . . the jury convicted him only on the charges that he acted alone).

In his book, *A Crime of Self Defense*, Prof. George Fletcher, thoughtfully adds: "Although jury nullification seems to stand in conflict with the rule of law [still] careful reflection underscores the power of the jury not to defeat the law, but to perfect the law, to realize the law's inherent values!"

The Origins of the American Bill of Rights

The U.S. Constitution as it was originally created and submitted to the colonies for ratification in 1787 did not include what we now call the Bill of Rights. This omission was the cause of much controversy as Americans debated whether to accept the new Constitution and the new federal government it created. One of the main concerns voiced by opponents of the document was that it lacked a detailed listing of guarantees of certain fundamental individual rights. These critics did not succeed in preventing the Constitution's ratification, but were in large part responsible for the existence of the Bill of Rights.

In 1787 the United States consisted of thirteen former British colonies that had been loosely bound since 1781 by the Articles of Confederation. Since declaring their independence from Great Britain in 1776, the former colonies had established their own colonial governments and constitutions, eight of which had bills of rights written into them. One of the most influential was Virginia's Declaration of Rights. Drafted largely by planter and legislator George Mason in 1776, the seventeen-point document combined philosophical declarations of natural rights with specific limitations on the powers of government. It served as a model for other state constitutions.

The sources for these declarations of rights included English law traditions dating back to the 1215 Magna Carta and the 1689 English Bill of Rights—two historic documents that provided specific legal guarantees of the "true, ancient, and indubitable rights and liberties of the people" of England. Other legal sources included the colonies' original charters, which declared that colonists should have the same "privileges, franchises, and immunities" that they would if they lived in England. The ideas concerning natural rights developed by John Locke and other English philosophers were also influential. Some of these concepts of rights had been cited in the Declaration of Independence to justify the American Revolution.

Unlike the state constitutions, the Articles of Confederation, which served as the national constitution from 1781 to 1788, lacked a bill of rights. Because the national government under the Articles of Confederation had little authority by design, most people believed it posed little threat to civil liberties, rendering a bill of rights unnecessary. However, many influential leaders criticized the very weakness of the national government for creating its own problems; it did not create an effective system for conducting a coherent foreign policy, settling disputes between states, printing money, and coping with internal unrest.

It was against this backdrop that American political leaders convened in Philadelphia in May 1787 with the stated intent to amend the Articles of Confederation. Four months later the Philadelphia Convention, going beyond its original mandate, created a whole new Constitution with a stronger national government. But while the new Constitution included a few provisions protecting certain civil liberties, it did not include any language similar to Virginia's Declaration of Rights. Mason, one of the delegates in Philadelphia, refused to sign the document. He listed his objections in an essay that began:

> There is no Declaration of Rights, and the Laws of the general government being paramount to the laws and constitution of the several States, the Declaration of Rights in the separate States are no security.

Mason's essay was one of hundreds of pamphlets and other writings produced as the colonists debated whether to ratify the new Constitution (nine of the thirteen colonies had to officially ratify the Constitution for it to go into effect). The supporters of the newly drafted Constitution became known as Federalists, while the loosely organized group of opponents were called Antifederalists. Antifederalists opposed the new Constitution for several reasons. They believed the presidency would create a monarchy. Congress would not be truly representative of the people, and state governments would be endangered. However, the argument that proved most effective was that the new document lacked a bill of rights and thereby threatened Americans with the loss of cherished individual liberties. Federalists realized that to gain the support of key states such as New York and Virginia, they needed to pledge to offer amendments to the Constitution that would be added immediately after its ratification. Indeed, it was not until this promise was made that the requisite number of colonies ratified the document. Massachusetts, Virginia, South Carolina, New Hampshire, and New York all included amendment recommendations as part of their decisions to ratify.

One of the leading Federalists, James Madison of Virginia, who was elected to the first Congress to convene under the new Constitution, took the lead in drafting the promised amendments. Under the process provided for in the Constitution, amendments needed to be passed by both the Senate and House of Representatives and then ratified by three-fourths of the states. Madison sifted through the suggestions provided by the states and drew upon the Virginia Declaration of Rights and other state documents in composing twelve amendments, which he introduced to Congress in September 1789. "If they are incorporated into the constitution," he argued in a speech introducing his proposed amendments,

> Independent tribunals of justice will consider themselves in a peculiar manner the guardians of those rights; they will be an impenetrable bulwark against every assumption of power in the legislative or executive; they will be naturally led to resist every encroachment upon rights expressly stipulated for in the constitution by the declaration of rights.

After debate and some changes to Madison's original proposals, Congress approved the twelve amendments and sent them to the states for ratification. Two amendments were not ratified; the remaining ten became known as the Bill of Rights. Their ratification by the states was completed on December 15, 1791.

Supreme Court Cases Involving the Right to a Fair Trial

1880

Strauder v. West Virginia
The Court reversed the murder conviction of a black man tried by an all-white jury, finding that he had been denied a jury of his peers.

1876

United States v. Cruikshank
The Court dismissed the federal prosecution against men accused of lynching two black men. Among other reasons, the Court found that the crime of conspiracy with which the accused were charged was not specific enough, denying them their right to be informed of the charges against them. By sending the case back to the U.S. Circuit Court for the District of Louisiana, the Supreme Court seriously curtailed the federal government's ability to protect the rights of newly freed slaves.

1932

Powell v. Alabama
The Court reversed the convictions of several illiterate blacks who had been sentenced to death, without the assistance of counsel at trial, for the alleged rape of two white women. This verdict paved the way for the decision in *Gideon v. Wainwright* (1963).

1938

Johnson v. Zerbst
The Court reversed a conviction for possession of counterfeit money because the defendant had been denied his right to counsel. Although he had waived that right, the Court found that his waiver was not valid without the advice of counsel.

1942

Betts v. Brady

The Court upheld the defendant's robbery conviction although he was unrepresented by counsel at trial. The Court found that being represented by counsel was not a fundamental right and Maryland's policy of appointing counsel only in capital cases was fair and reasonable.

1948

In re Oliver

The Court reversed the decision in the case of a man who was convicted and incarcerated for contempt on the basis of his testimony before a one-man grand jury. The Court held that this procedure denied him the rights protected by the Sixth Amendment, including reasonable notice of the charges against him, the opportunity to call witnesses, and the assistance of counsel.

1963

Gideon v. Wainwright

The Court reversed the position of *Betts v. Brady* and held that all felony defendants are entitled to legal representation irrespective of the crime charged, and courts are to appoint an attorney if a defendant is too poor to hire one.

1965

Estes v. Texas

The defendant's conviction for swindling was reversed by the Court because allowing the trial to be carried on live television was prejudicial and unfair.

Pointer v. Texas

The Court reversed the robbery conviction because the complaining witness had never been cross-examined by counsel for the defendant.

1966

Sheppard v. Maxwell
The famous conviction of doctor Samuel Sheppard for murdering his wife was set aside on the finding that the judge "did not fulfill his duty to protect Sheppard from inherently prejudicial publicity which saturated the country."

1967

Klopfer v. North Carolina
The Court held that a North Carolina procedural device, whereby a defendant could remain subject to prosecution indefinitely, violated the right to a speedy trial.

Washington v. Texas
The Court struck down a Texas statute that prohibited a defendant accused of a crime from calling his coparticipant in the crime to testify in his defense. The Court found that the statute violated the defendant's Sixth Amendment right to have compulsory process for obtaining witnesses in his favor.

1968

Duncan v. Louisiana
The Court held that defendants have the right to a trial by jury in all criminal cases.

1970

Williams v. Florida
The Court ruled that the right to a trial by jury does not require that jury membership be fixed at twelve.

1972

Argesinger v. Hamlin
The Court reaffirmed that the decision in *Gideon v. Wainwright* guarantees an indigent the right to counsel for all offenses, not merely for those punishable by a jail term of more than six months.

Rabe v. Washington
The conviction of a defendant who showed a sexually explicit movie at a drive-in was overturned by the Court because the state obscenity statute under which he was convicted failed to provide fair notice that the location of the exhibition of obscenity was a vital element of the offense.

1977

Castaneda v. Partida
The Court found that intentional discrimination in the Texas grand jury selection process denied Mexican Americans the right to trial by a jury of peers.

1979

Gannett Co. v. DePasquale
The Court ruled that the press does not have a right to attend a trial over the objection of the defendants.

1984

Strickland v. Washington
The Court reversed a death sentence because the defense counsel's behavior was unreasonable, thus affirming that the Sixth Amendment right to counsel is the right to effective counsel.

1986

Batson v. Kentucky
The Court held that a black defendant is denied equal protection when he is tried before a jury from which members of his race have been purposely excluded.

1988

Coy v. Iowa
The Court reversed a conviction for child molestation because the witnesses testified behind a screen, violating the defendant's right to confront the witnesses against him.

Taylor v. Illinois
The Court held that the compulsory process clause of the Sixth Amendment was not violated by the exclusion from trial of a witness who had not appeared on the defendant's witness list submitted prior to trial.

United States v. Owens
The Court found that the confrontation clause is not violated by the admission of a prior, out-of-court identification of a witness who is unable, because of memory loss, to explain the basis of the identification.

1990

Maryland v. Craig
The Court found that the confrontation clause was not violated by allowing witnesses in a child abuse case to testify over closed-circuit television.

2001

Texas v. Cobb
The Court held that the right to counsel is "offense specific" and does not extend to additional offenses that are factually related to an original charge.

Books

Jeffrey Abramson, *We, the Jury: The Jury System and the Ideal of Democracy*. New York: BasicBooks, 1995.

Ellen Alderman and Caroline Kennedy, *In Our Defense*. New York: William Morrow. 1991.

Brian Barry, *Justice as Impartiality*. Oxford: Oxford University Press, 1996.

William Merritt Beaney, *The Right to Counsel in American Courts*. Westport, CT: Greenwood, 1972.

Norman F. Cantor, *Imagining the Law: Common Law and the Foundations of the American Legal System*. New York: HarperCollins, 1997.

J.S. Cockburn and Thomas A. Green, eds., *Twelve Good Men and True: The Criminal Trial Jury in England, 1200–1800*. Princeton: Princeton University Press, 1985.

David Cole and James X. Dempsey, *Terrorism and the Constitution: Sacrificing Civil Liberties in the Name of National Security*. New York: New Press, 2002.

Alan M. Dershowitz, *The Best Defense*. New York: Random House, 1982.

———, *Reasonable Doubts: The Criminal Justice System and the O.J. Simpson Case*. New York: Simon & Schuster, 1996.

Geoffrey Rudolph Elton, *Star Chamber Stories*. New York: Barnes & Noble, 1974.

Myron Farber, *Someone Is Lying*. New York: Doubleday, 1982.

Michel Foucault, *Discipline and Punish: The Birth of the Prison*. London: Penguin, 1977.

Lawrence Meir Friedman, *Crime and Punishment in American History*. New York, BasicBooks, 1994.

————, *A History of American Law*. New York: Simon & Schuster, 1985.

Learned Hand, *The Bill of Rights*. Cambridge, MA: Harvard University Press, 1958.

Francis Howard Heller, *The Sixth Amendment to the Constitution of the United States: A Study in Constitutional History*. Lawrence: University of Kansas Press, 1969.

Nat Hentoff, *Living the Bill of Rights: How to Be an Authentic American*. New York: HarperCollins, 1998.

Peter Irons, *Brennan vs. Rhenquist: The Battle for the Constitution*. New York: Alfred A. Knopf, 1994.

Harry Kalven and Hans Zeisel, *The American Jury*. Chicago: University of Chicago Press, 1987.

Yale Kamisar, Wayne H. LaFave, and Jerold H. Israel, *Modern Criminal Procedure*. St. Paul, MN: West, 1990.

Edward W. Knappman, ed., *Great American Trials: From Salem Witchcraft to Rodney King*. Canton, MI: Invisible Ink, 1993.

Max Lerner, *Nine Scorpions in a Bottle: Great Judges and Cases of the Supreme Court*. New York: Arcade, 1994.

Earl M. Maltz, ed., *Rhenquist Justice: Understanding the Court Dynamic*. Lawrence: University of Kansas Press, 2003.

Matt Matravers, *Justice and Punishment: The Rationale of Coercion*. Oxford: Oxford University Press, 2000.

Lloyd E. Moore, *The Jury: Tool of Kings, Palladium of Liberty*. Cincinnati, OH: Anderson, 1988.

Frederick Pollack and Frederic William Maitland, *The History of English Law Before the Time of Edward I*. London: Cambridge University Press, 1968.

Bernard Schwartz, *The Great Rights of Mankind: A History of the American Bill of Rights*. New York: Oxford University Press, 1977.

Laurence H. Tribe, *God Save This Honorable Court: How the Choice of the Supreme Court Justices Shapes Our History*. New York: Random House, 1985.

Charles H. Whitebread, *Criminal Procedure*. New York: Foundation Press, 2000.

John Maxcy Zane, *The Story of Law*. Indianapolis: Liberty Fund, 1998.

Web Sites

Famous Trials, www.umkc.edu/famoustrials. This site offers extensive information about famous trials from ancient Greece to O.J. Simpson.

Findlaw, www.Findlaw.com. The most comprehensive legal Web site for lawyers, law students, and the public. It offers assistance in finding a lawyer as well as full citations of cases from state and federal courts, articles about current legal issues, and a marketplace for legal products.

FreedomLaw.com, www.freedomlaw.com. Maintained by a not-for-profit libertarian organization, this thought-provoking Web site provides information about civil liberties abuses and a self-help legal clinic.